DEFIANTLY JOYFUL

DEFIANTLY JOYFUL

UNITARIAN UNIVERSALIST LGBTQIA+ HISTORIES

DIANA K. MCLEAN, EDITOR

Skinner House Books
Boston

 Published by Skinner House Books, 24 Farnsworth St., Boston, MA 02210–1409.

skinnerhouse.org

Printed in the United States

Cover design by Jeenee Lee
Text design by Tim Holtz

print ISBN: 978-1-55896-978-0
eBook ISBN: 978-1-55896-979-7

5 4 3 2 1
29 28 27 26

CIP on file with the Library of Congress.

Contents

A Note About Language

Many words and acronyms have been used to describe the spectrum of gender identities and sexual orientations, and people's terminology is affected by many factors, including historical context. Rather than try to standardize such terms across this book, I have chosen to leave each author's language as it was offered to me, respecting each author's right to identify themself and speak about their communities in the way that is most authentic to them. When using other sources, such as for the timeline or appendices, I left the acronyms as they appear in the original documents. So, for example, I use *LGBTQIA+* in the preface and postscript, but contributors have sometimes used other versions of that acronym. Some have used *gay* as an umbrella term; I would probably use *queer*, because the term *gay* has typically been used to refer to people (sometimes only men) who are attracted to the same gender, which can lead to the invisibilizing of bi+ and trans+ folx. At the same time, I know that some people dislike the word *queer* because of its historical and ongoing use as a slur. There is no single right answer because the community represented by those words is not a monolith.

For example, contributor Sandra Szelag provided this explanation with her submission:

> In 1971, *gay* referred to lesbians, bisexual people, crossdressers, transgender people and everyone who wasn't straight and cisgender. Neither the general public nor the "gay" community had much language for what we now consider a variety

> of sexual orientations and gender identities, although the phrase *gays* and *bisexuals* was sometimes used and the word *lesbian* was becoming more common, partly as a result of the influence of lesbian feminists. The word *gay* also served as an alternative to the generally used term *homosexual*, which was fraught with connotations of serious mental illness. The use of that term was definitely not acceptable to us and only served to indicate the depth of the problem.

This means that you may encounter wording that is not what you yourself are familiar with, use, or prefer. My hope is that even if you find yourself taken aback by a contributor's language, you will be able to bring curiosity to the different language choices contributors use—particularly if they bring up strong reactions in you—and make space for different definitions and experiences of the many identity terms used in these pages.

Preface

Unitarian Universalists, individually and collectively, have often been at the forefront of LGBTQIA+ justice efforts. We were among the first religious organizations to conduct same-sex services of union. We were among the first to ordain openly gay male clergy, and later openly lesbian, bisexual, and transgender clergy. We responded with love rather than hate to the AIDS crisis. We were leaders in the fight for marriage equality in a variety of states and at the national level.

Our shared Unitarian Universalist values, outlined in Article II of the bylaws of the Unitarian Universalist Association, as updated in 2024, includes the statement "We declare that every person is inherently worthy and has the right to flourish with dignity, love, and compassion." (The previous section of that section of bylaws, the Unitarian Universalist Principles, began by affirming "the inherent worth and dignity of every person.") We have demonstrated for decades that "every person" certainly includes LGBTQIA+ folks.

It is equally true, however, that we have not been perfect in this area. My wife and I are both Unitarian Universalist women ministers—a queer clergy couple, something that just a generation ago might have been unthinkable even in our liberal denomination. When I came out in 2014, I didn't worry at all about losing either the faith to which I had belonged since childhood or my position as ministerial intern at a Unitarian Universalist congregation. My colleagues in ministry did not have that safety just a few decades ago, during the same years that my family was discovering Unitarian Universalism. I do not remember any openly LGBTQIA+ people in my childhood church, and I now realize that, even in a liberal religious setting like ours, being out might not have felt safe in 1970s–80s Nebraska. I was sobered to realize that only within my lifetime has our liberal denomination begun to consider the humanity and rights of LGBTQIA+ folks—and not always compassionately. I also recognize that as a white woman, my queer identity is still more readily accepted than some others.

There are barriers to full inclusion even today, particularly for trans and nonbinary people. Clergy and other religious professionals, in particular, have often found it hard to find and keep congregational positions. The barriers are still more complex for people who are marginalized on more than one axis of identity, such as sexual orientation and race, or gender identity and neurotype. We have made progress, but there is still work to do.

This book tells some stories of how LGBTQIA+ lives and Unitarian Universalist faith have intersected, at personal, congregational, and denominational levels. It also illustrates times when our faith helped to transform the lives of LGBTQIA+ people. The stories captured here often moved me to tears—sometimes tears of sorrow for the harm done to individuals, and sometimes tears of pride in Unitarian Universalists for taking faithful risks to further the cause of LGBTQIA+ justice and inclusion.

This book is part of a larger project, the UU Rainbow History Project, sponsored by the UU Retired Ministers and Partners Association (UURMaPA) and partially funded by a grant from the UU Funding Program. The project began as a recognition of the fiftieth anniversary of the Stonewall Rebellion and includes a website (uurainbowhistory.net), two conferences held in 2019, and now this book.

The larger project focuses on the history and stories of LGBTQIA+ ministers, their partners, and their allies. This book presents the voices of LGBTQIA+ folks themselves, not only ministers, but also other religious professionals and lay members of congregations. It contains primarily personal essays, together with some reprinted sermons and other historical documents—which also often touch on the personal, just as personal essays touch on historical moments. I chose not to include material that is already available on the Rainbow History website, and I am grateful for all the excellent submissions that I received. I encourage readers to go beyond this volume by visiting the website and reading what's available there: not only additional personal essays and sermons, but also transcripts of panel discussions, keynotes, and more. It is a rich resource for anyone wanting to know more about LGBTQIA+ lived experiences within Unitarian Universalism.

This history is still being written, as we continue to resist efforts to limit LGBTQIA+ rights. My hope is that this book will inspire us by showing both our successes and our failures as we have imperfectly lived into our affirmation of the inherent worthiness of every person, and have imperfectly included LGBTQIA+ people in that affirmation. There is much more material still out there, and I hope that it will be published in another project.

Contributors to this book lived through some of the key episodes in our denominational history. As with all memory and all history, their accounts may sometimes differ. I invite you to set aside any inclination to decide whose version is "right" or "wrong," and to focus instead on the larger messages in each essay.

Even as I prepare this text, we are losing LGBTQIA+ trailblazers, including Rev. Dr. Dorothy Emerson, who was key to this project, and I was brought on board after her death. During the writing of the book we lost at least a dozen others. These deaths and others made even more clear that we must capture this history before we lose it.

However, no single book can contain all the relevant stories. Moreover, no one owes us their stories: not the "us" behind this book project, nor the "us" of the book's eventual audience. With that clarity, I have honored both an explicit "no" and silence in response to requests for stories. If, in doing so, I have inadvertently omitted anyone who would have wished to say "yes" to the request, I offer a heartfelt apology.

This book is inevitably an incomplete collection, only a sampling of the stories that are out there, some known and some relatively unknown. Not everyone who could share a story wants to; not all the stories still have people who are alive to tell them. I've done my best, and yet I know that pieces will always be missing.

Given that, I have worked to make this book as representative as possible of the stories I know are out there. While each contribution is unique, it also stands for many others, similar in a variety of ways, that did not make it into these pages. I hope that, together, they will reinforce the understanding that LGBTQIA+ folks, even within a single faith tradition, are far from being a monolith about whom broad generalizations can be made.

Historical Context

Some readers may not be familiar enough with LGBTQIA+ history to know the contexts in which the stories collected here take place. An overview of that history could easily fill a book of its own, but I offer here a timeline of some of its most important events in North America and within Unitarian Universalism. If you are interested in more information on the UUA's official positions over the years, the appendix lists the LGBTQIA+ resolutions passed at General Assembly since 1970.

Context is also important in understanding Unitarian Universalist positions on LGBTQIA+ issues across time—in this case, the context of how some other religious traditions approached issues of LGBTQIA+ justice and inclusion. That topic could also be a book in itself, so for this introduction, I will stick to a quick summary of some of the most prominent religious stances that have influenced a wide segment of mainstream culture in the United States and Canada.

Same-sex desire and gender nonconformity have been understood in a vast diversity of ways in different eras by different religions. In the countries and eras in which Unitarianism and Universalism first developed, same-sex sexual acts were understood primarily through a moral lens and were often criminalized as sinful. In the late nineteenth century science and religion diverged in their understandings of same-sex attraction and gender nonconformity—Abrahamic religions continued to view them as a matter of sin, while sexologists started viewing them as a pathology. It wasn't until the mid-twentieth century that homosexuality became politicized, most notably by US Senator Joseph McCarthy, who framed homosexuals as a threat to national security. This created the impetus for early gay rights organizing. Increasing state and religious repression came to a head in the late 1960s, when LGBTQIA+ people fought back against criminalization and police brutality. The Stonewall Rebellion of 1969 sparked a new liberation movement—and it, in turn, sparked a new anti-gay movement based in conservative Christian beliefs. By the late 1970s, many evangelical churches made the denunciation of homosexuality a cornerstone of their dogma and their politics. Their positions were based in inaccurate Biblical interpretation, but nonetheless became (and remain) a crucial influence on right-leaning politics in the US, Canada, and other countries.

As LGBTQIA+ people worked for justice in legal, political, educational, and social settings, they also organized against anti-gay bigotry in religion. The late 1960s and 1970s saw a proliferation of LGBTQIA+ groups within mainstream traditions and also the creation of explicitly LGBTQIA+ denominations, such as Metropolitan Community Churches. In many traditions, advocacy has resulted in LGBTQIA+ inclusion, but these gains have always been a site of struggle. For example, thousands of congregations left the United Methodist Church in 2022 over its continued rejection of same-sex marriage and refusal to ordain LGBTQIA+ clergy. Conversely, the Episcopal Church, the Evangelical Lutheran Church in America, and the Presbyterian Church (USA) began ordaining LGBTQIA+ clergy and lost congregations that did not support that action.

Although LGBTQIA+ people have been members and leaders within Unitarianism, Universalism, and Unitarian Universalism since the very beginnings of our faith movement, and although Unitarian Universalism is now well known for its inclusion of and advocacy for LGBTQIA+ people, our history on this topic is complex. The first General Assembly resolution related to LGBTQIA+ issues was passed in 1970, but only three years previously a survey had found that 88 percent of Unitarian Universalists thought that homosexuality should be discouraged. In 1973, advocacy by gay, lesbian, and bisexual UU leaders resulted in the establishment of an official UUA office dedicated to gay concerns—an enormous achievement—but for the next fifteen years, adequate funding and staffing for that office was the subject of almost continuous debate.

In 1987, the UUA established the Common Vision Planning Committee, a diverse group of clergy and laity from around North America tasked with collecting information about how welcomed and accepted gay, lesbian, and bisexual people felt in Unitarian Universalist congregations. (It would be another decade before the denomination would begin attending to trans inclusion as well.) The committee published a report that exposed many negative attitudes, deep prejudices, and profound ignorance about bisexual, gay, and lesbian people, which resulted in their exclusion from UU congregations. This reality troubled many people who were committed to making UU congregations welcoming and inclusive places for all people, especially groups who experience exclusion, discrimination, and misrepresentation within our society. Citing the inherent worth and dignity of every person, the 1989 General Assembly voted to initiate the Welcoming Congregation program recommended by the Common Vision Planning Committee.

Over the next three decades, the majority of Unitarian Universalist congregations went through an intentional process of becoming recognized Welcoming Congregations, and UU leaders, laypeople, congregations, and institutions became increasingly active in campaigns for LGBTQIA+ justice. Yet for too many people, the struggles continue—both in our wider world and within UU spaces. By 2018, more than 75 percent of congregations were recognized as Welcoming Congregations but a denominational survey conducted that year found that 72 percent of trans Unitarian Universalists did not feel that their congregation was completely inclusive of them. There will always be more work to do to live out our values more fully.

History is often told as a narrative of steady linear progress, which obscures the complexity of movements for justice, but the timeline that follows (and this book as a whole) strives to render visible both the victories and the struggles of LGBTQIA+ Unitarian Universalists, as well as the very long history of LGBTQIA+ leaders and activism within Unitarian Universalism and the role of Unitarian Universalism within larger LGBTQIA+ movements. This timeline focuses largely on events of significance on denominational, national, and LGBTQIA+ movement levels, but I hope it inspires you to explore and help document this history even further.

Timeline

Compiled by Rev. Diana McLean and Alex Kapitan, with gratitude to participants at Unitarian Universalist Retired Ministers and Partners conferences in 2019 and others who were consulted.

Events in regular font took place within Unitarian Universalism; those in bold are more general.

1833	Augustus Graham, a Unitarian businessman, social activist, philanthropist, and life partner of John Bell Graham, becomes a founding member of the First Unitarian Church of Brooklyn, NY. In 1851, his is the first funeral held in the church's new 1844 building, and he leaves generous bequests to further Unitarianism.
1868	Rev. Phebe Coffin Hanaford is ordained as a Universalist minister. Hannaford is publicly partnered with Ellen Miles for 44 years, through all four of her pastorates. At the First Universalist Church of Jersey City, NJ, Miles runs the Sunday school and local newspapers refer to her as "the minister's wife." Hanaford is very active in the women's rights movement and officiates the funerals of Elizabeth Cady Stanton and Susan B. Anthony.
1893	Rev. Marion Murdoch and Rev. Florence Buck are called to the First Unitarian Church of Cleveland, where they serve as co-ministers. The two are dedicated life partners and part of the Iowa Sisterhood of feminist Unitarian women ministers. Buck later works in the American Unitarian Association's department of religious education and makes major contributions to expanding religious education to all.

1897 ***Sexual Inversion*** **by Havelock Ellis and John Addington Symonds is published. The book represents a shift toward considering homosexuality in scientific and medical terms rather than solely in moral terms.**

The first printing of *Sexual Inversion* includes an (anonymized) essay by James Mills Peirce, a Harvard math professor and former Unitarian minister. Referred to as "perhaps the strongest defense of homosexuality written by an American in the 19th century," the essay makes the radical argument that homosexuality should be considered just as normal, natural, and moral as heterosexuality.

1917 Dr. Alan Hart (as he comes to be known) receives the first documented gender-affirming surgery in the US (a hysterectomy). He goes on to pioneer the use of X-rays in tuberculosis detection, which likely saves millions of lives. Hart and his wife Edna Ruddick Hart move to Hartford, CT, in the 1940s and become leaders in the First Unitarian Congregational Society of Hartford (now the Unitarian Society of Hartford). They live their lives together without anyone knowing Hart's gender history.

1924 Dr. Martha May Eliot is hired by the US Children's Bureau, where she works for 30 years, eventually becoming its chief. She and her life partner Ethel Collins Dunham both hold MDs from Johns Hopkins Medical School and teach pediatrics at Yale. Eliot makes major contributions to maternal, child, and public health. Her sister, Abigail Adams Eliot, a leader in the field of early childhood education, also has a female life partner: Anna Holman. The Eliots' Unitarian faith informs their lifelong devotion to children's well-being.

1934 **The US Motion Picture Association starts enforcing the Hays Code, which effectively prevents any positive portrayals of homosexuality or gender nonconformity on screen for decades.**

1945	Rev. Charles Vickery, a gay man (although not out), is ordained as a Universalist minister. He later becomes program director of volunteer services for the newly merged Unitarian Universalist Service Committee and the first settled minister of the UU fellowship in Mexico City, Asociación Unitaria Mexicana, where, in 1970, he starts what may be the first gay awareness group in a UU congregation.
1948	**Alfred Kinsey publishes the first of his two revolutionary books on human sexuality, showing that same-sex sexual attraction is far more common than previously believed and arguing that sexuality is a spectrum, not a binary.**
1950	**US Senator Joseph McCarthy gives a speech to Congress that ramps up the campaign to oust suspected homosexual federal employees. By the end of the decade, the "Lavender Scare" results in as many as 10,000 workers being fired or forced to resign.** **The Mattachine Society, the biggest US gay rights organization of the mid-twentieth century, is founded.**
1953	Rev. Wallace de Ortega Maxey, minister of the First Universalist Church of Los Angeles and member of the Mattachine Society, hosts the society's pivotal first two conventions at the church. Maxey lives with his partner Robert Hernandez Deanda in the rectory and starts a gay- and bisexual-friendly singles group at the church with Mattachine cofounder Chuck Rowland. Church members complain about Maxey to Universalist officials and file a complaint with the FBI, and he resigns in 1954.
1957	Rev. Ernest Pipes Jr., a Unitarian minister in Santa Monica, CA, performs the first documented same-sex wedding in Unitarian Universalism.

1965	Rev. Richard Nash is hired by the Unitarian Universalist Service Committee, later becoming its director of community services. He becomes a trailblazer for LGBTQIA+ liberation within the UUA.
1966	**The Compton's Cafeteria riot takes place in San Francisco, part of the growing resistance to police brutality and criminalization of gay and transgender people.**
1967	The UU Committee on Goals publishes the results of a survey on beliefs and attitudes within the denomination, finding that 88% of UUs believe homosexuality should be discouraged, 12% believe it should not be discouraged, and 0.1% believe it should be encouraged.
1969	**The Stonewall Rebellion takes place in New York City, sparking the gay liberation movement.** Zazu Nova, a Black transgender Unitarian teen, is part of the vanguard at Stonewall. Nova goes on to become a member of STAR (Street Transvestite Action Revolutionaries, founded by Marsha P. Johnson and Sylvia Rivera), and a founding member of New York Gay Youth, one of the first LGBT youth organizations in the US. Rev. James L. Stoll, who has previously served the UU church in Kennewick, WA, for seven years, publicly declares himself to be homosexual, one of the first ordained ministers in North America to do so. He begins advocating for gay rights in Unitarian Universalism and the wider world in articles and sermons. Stoll goes on to found the first counseling center for gays and lesbians in San Francisco.
1970	UUA General Assembly passes a General Resolution condemning discrimination against homosexuals and bisexuals, the first General Assembly resolution to address LGBTQIA+ issues, thanks to the efforts of gay UU leaders.

	Arlington Street Church in Boston increasingly becomes a community hub for gay organizing, providing space for groups such as the Homophile Union of Boston, the Boston chapter of Daughters of Bilitis, the Homophile Community Health Services Center, and Boston UU Gays and Lesbians.
1971	At General Assembly, Rev. Richard Nash and Elgin Blair found the UU Gay Caucus and begin lobbying for the creation of an Office of Gay Affairs. The UUA publishes About Your Sexuality (AYS), a comprehensive sexuality education program for junior high students, which asserts that homosexuality is acceptable. In 1973, a new unit on homosexuality is added. Rev. Frank Robertson, an out gay man, is called by All Souls Unitarian Church in Washington, DC, as minister of religious education, a role he holds for 10 years. In 1977, he is elected to the UUA Board of Trustees. He is a lifelong advocate for LGBTQIA+ liberation in the UUA and wider world.
1972	The UUA publishes *The Invisible Minority*, created by Deryck Calderwood and Wasyl Sykodzinsky, an audiovisual study program about changing societal views of homosexuality that invites participants to inform themselves and honor the worth and dignity of all people regardless of sexual orientation.
1973	General Assembly passes a General Resolution to create a UUA Office on Gay Affairs, if funds can be found outside the existing denominational budget. It is to be staffed by gay people and be a resource to the UUA. The UUA board votes to establish, but not fund, the Office of Gay Affairs, and it is rank-ordered 42nd out of 45 new proposals. On instructions from UUA President Bob West, the board also removes the office's function of advocacy and the requirement that its staff be gay.

The Charles Street Meetinghouse, a UU congregation in the then-gay neighborhood of Boston's Beacon Hill, begins hosting a gay coffeehouse, out of which grows *Gay Community News*, the long-running "paper of record" for the gay liberation movement. In 1974 John Kyper, a UU and writer for the paper, is deported from Canada due to carrying copies of *GCN*, which becomes a catalyst for the repeal of the law banning homosexuals from entering the country.

1974 Rev. Norm Naylor, UU minister in Winnipeg, Manitoba, officiates the first documented same-sex wedding in Canada.

The agenda for the UUA board meeting includes a modest $6,000 line item to fund the Office of Gay Affairs. At the next board meeting, Sandy Szelag and Henry Wiemhoff, co-coordinators of the UU Gay Caucus, make another effort to fund the office, which also fails.

At General Assembly, Rev. Frank Robertson moves to fund the Office of Gay Concerns (OGC) at $38,500 by cutting two other programs that had been among the 45 proposals in January. This passes: General Assembly votes to urge the board to fund the OGC.

The UUA board votes 12 to 11 to fund the OGC in accordance with the GA Business Resolution.

President Bob West publishes a front-page article in *UU World* opposing the OGC and calling for a reordering of priorities.

1975 Arlie Scott, a lesbian, is hired as UUA Director of Gay Affairs, but is not accepted by other staff, some of whom refuse to ride in the elevator with her.

At General Assembly, a resolution to close the Office of Gay Concerns is defeated 257–402.

The UUA board funds the OGC for only half of the coming year.

The UU Gay Caucus collaborates with AYS trainers to train gay and lesbian folks to lead AYS courses in their churches.

1977 **Anita Bryant begins her Save Our Children campaign, which becomes a flashpoint for anti-gay hatred and spurs organized, nationwide US opposition to the gay liberation movement.**

Partly in response to the Save Our Children campaign, General Assembly passes a Business Resolution urging UUs to fight against persecution and intolerance of gay people.

UUA President Paul Carnes expresses his intention to cut the position of director of the OGC to half-time.

At a UUA board meeting, Rev. Frank Robertson shares the fact that he was refused appointment to the Youth Adult Committee because of prejudice against him as a gay man. (Carnes has admitted this in a small gathering of UUA board members.) Robertson requests that his statement be on the record, but it never appears in the board minutes.

The UUA board reduces the staffing of the OGC by hiring Rev. Bob Wheatley as both its director and the half-time director of the Committee on Aging. This move is opposed by the Advisory Committee to the OGC. Wheatley comes out when he takes the OGC job.

1978 **Harvey Milk, one of the first openly gay elected officials in the US, is murdered.**

Gilbert Baker designs the rainbow flag (as requested by Harvey Milk prior to his assassination).

Anne Heller and Mark (Marco) Belletini, as students, lead a chapel service at Starr King School for the Ministry on "Coming Out."

1979	**Jerry Falwell, president of the Moral Majority, speaks out against homosexuality and begins to organize a march on DC by the Christian right, scheduled for April 1980. UUs oppose him in coalition with others.** The first out gay UU ministers are called to serve congregations as senior ministers: Rev. Douglas Morgan Strong is called to All Souls Church, Augusta, ME, and Rev. Mark (Marco) Belletini is called to the First Unitarian Universalist Society of San Francisco as an interim associate minister. First UU Society of San Francisco also calls Barbara Pescan, a lesbian, and Mark Mosher DeWolfe, a gay man, as intern ministers. Beacon Press publishes *The Transsexual Empire: The Making of the She-Male* by Janice Raymond, an extremely influential book that frames trans women as an enemy of the women's rights movement and launches anti-trans feminism.
1980	General Assembly passes a Business Resolution urging Unitarian Universalists, the UUA, and the Unitarian Universalist Ministers Association (UUMA) to assist in the settlement of openly gay, lesbian, and bisexual ministers. Erinn Melby publicly declares that she is transsexual as a student at Starr King School for the Ministry during a presentation on gays, lesbians, and transsexuals, having first come out as trans in 1967. Denied fellowship by the Ministerial Fellowship Committee in 1984 and 1985, she is finally passed in 1994 and ordained in 1995. A handful of other trans ministers are also ordained in the '80s and '90s.
1981	**The first official report on what will become known as the AIDS epidemic is published. Highly publicized and stigmatized as a "gay disease," AIDS will kill more than 40,000 people in the US within six years.** From the early days of the epidemic, the First Unitarian Universalist Church of San Diego ministers to the sick. It holds annual Thanksgiving feasts for people with AIDS and their

caregivers and offers loving, supportive memorial services and celebrations of life.

Rev. Mark Mosher DeWolfe is called by the Unitarian Congregation of South Peel, now the Unitarian Congregation in Mississauga, Ontario. During his seven-year ministry the congregation flourishes. DeWolfe dies in 1988 at the age of 35 from an AIDS-related illness.

1982 **Wisconsin becomes the first US state to prohibit discrimination based on sexual orientation in employment, housing, or public accommodations.**

Rev. Eugene B. Navias, an out gay man, is promoted by UUA President Eugene Pickett to become the director of the UUA's Religious Education Department (having served as a religious education field consultant since 1963). His many contributions to UU religious education include championing AYS, developing the UUA's accreditation program for DREs, and editing the UUA's religious education packet on AIDS. He is invited to give the prestigious Berry Street Essay in 1983; his is probably the first to mention gays and lesbians.

1984 The UUA Department of Ministry and the Affirmative Action Committee invite gay and lesbian ministers to a gathering in Oakland, CA, at which the idea for a national or continental conference is discussed.

General Assembly passes a Business Resolution affirming the practice of UU clergy performing services of union for same-sex couples and requesting that the Department of Ministerial and Congregational Services develop and distribute supporting materials for both religious professionals and laypeople.

Charlie Howard, a gay man, is murdered by teenagers shouting homophobic slurs as he walks home from the Unitarian Church of Bangor, ME, with his boyfriend.

1985	An estimated 50–100 LGB Unitarian Universalists and a few allies gather at the First Unitarian Church of Houston, one of the few UU churches served by an openly gay minister (Rev. Bob Schaibly), for the first convocation of Unitarian Universalists for Lesbian and Gay Concerns (UULGC), previously the UU Gay Caucus. With this gathering, the grassroots movement of gay and lesbian UUs becomes a national presence.
1986	The First Unitarian Church of San Diego hosts the second UULGC convocation, titled "Together in the Struggle." About a hundred people attend, from 21 states and Canada. UUA President William Schulz, Executive Vice President Kay Montgomery, and Director for Social Responsibility Loretta Williams are featured speakers. The program includes plenary sessions, worship services, and workshops on topics including AIDS, homophobia, religious education, and starting local chapters of UULGC. A motion urging the UUA and UUMA boards to foster specialized AIDS ministries and education passes unanimously. Attendees also request that the UUA increase the staffing of the Office of Lesbian and Gay Concerns to two full-time staff and give $2,000 to assist in paying for those positions. The convocation is preceded by a one-day gathering of gay, lesbian, and bisexual UU ministers. At this time there are approximately a hundred LGB ministers serving in UU parish ministry, but only six are publicly out as gay or lesbian. General Assembly passes a General Resolution opposing AIDS discrimination and urging Unitarian Universalists to support the civil rights of people with AIDS. Rev. Jay Deacon is hired as the director of what is now called the Office of Lesbian and Gay Concerns (OLGC). The UUA board appoints an AIDS Advisory Panel, which recommends the formation of an AIDS Action Working Group. The UUA amends its personnel manual to bar discrimination against people with HIV.

1987	The OLGC coordinates UU participation in a march on Washington to protest the US Supreme Court decision in *Bowers v. Hardwick* the previous year, which upholds the constitutionality of a Georgia sodomy law criminalizing oral and anal sex in private between consenting adults. Unitarian Universalists come from all over the country, holding a worship service at All Souls Unitarian Church in DC and a circle dance, led by Starhawk, before attending the protest. 800 protesters are arrested, and the court personnel who handle them wear rubber gloves. General Assembly passes a Business Resolution calling on UUs to work to overturn legislation restricting LGB rights and to boycott the products and services of organizations that discriminate on the basis of sexual orientation. In his report to General Assembly, President Schulz wholeheartedly encourages congregations to accept gay and lesbian people.
1988	The UUA's Common Vision Planning Committee surveys UU attitudes toward homosexuality. It finds that while the majority of UUs feel positively toward LGB people, significant numbers do not, and a minority are extremely hostile toward LGB people. Almost half of heterosexual respondents express reservations at the idea of having an LGB minister, and similar numbers wrote that LGB people had a mental illness that could be treated, or that they could be "cured" by conversion programs. Anti-LGB comments submitted by respondents stun the UUA board in early 1989 when the committee presents its report and recommendations.
1989	The UUA's Beyond Categorical Thinking workshops begin, teaching congregations to avoid discrimination in calling ministers. General Assembly passes resolutions to (a) establish a Welcoming Congregation program to combat homophobia in UU congregations and to educate UUs about sexual

orientation, (b) oppose discriminatory practices toward people with AIDS/HIV and expand educational programs about HIV and clean needle programs, and (c) condemn the Helms Amendment restricting the ability of people with HIV to enter the US.

1990 The Welcoming Congregation program is launched with the publication of *The Welcoming Congregation Handbook*, written by Bobbie Harro, which contains action items, guidance, and 10 workshops.

1991 The UU Bisexual Network is founded by Bobbi Keppel and Alan Hamilton.

First Parish Brewster Unitarian Universalist, Brewster, MA, becomes the first recognized Welcoming Congregation.

1992 **Brandon Teena, a young transgender man, is murdered along with two companions in Humboldt, NE, due to being trans. His story becomes nationally known in 1999 with the release of the film *Boys Don't Cry*.**

A ballot measure in Oregon seeks to prohibit laws that would ban discrimination on the basis of sexual orientation. Opponents organize under the slogan "No on 9" and roundly defeat it, although similar measures later pass in a few Oregon counties.

The Pacific Northwest District of the UUA and the UUMA raise $5,000 for the No on 9 campaign, and First Unitarian Portland, under the leadership of Rev. Marilyn Sewell, wraps itself entirely in ribbon to support the campaign.

Rev. Meg Riley, director of the OLGC, leads a continental Welcoming Congregation training. Facilitator teams are chosen for racial diversity. Bisexuality awareness, which is not explicitly included in the 1990 handbook, is also included.

The UUA board passes a resolution expressing disapproval of the Boy Scouts of America's policy of discrimination against gay and atheist scouts and leaders.

General Assembly passes a Resolution of Immediate Witness opposing the legalization of LGB discrimination against gays, lesbians, and bisexuals, in response to hate campaigns in Oregon and Colorado.

The LREDA fall conference in Cazenovia, NY, challenges religious educators to create programs that address gay and lesbian concerns.

Dee Graham, as a student, teaches a class on lesbian and gay spirituality at Starr King School for the Ministry, likely the first time this topic is taught in any of the schools of the Graduate Theological Union.

1993 **Minnesota becomes the first US state to prohibit discrimination based on gender identity or sexual orientation. No other state will comprehensively protect transgender people from discrimination until Rhode Island in 2001.**

Stan Calder, an out gay man, becomes president of the board of the Canadian Unitarian Council. He is a lifelong advocate for LGBTQIA+ liberation within the CUC.

At a convocation in Columbus, OH, UULGC merges with the UU Bisexual Network to form Interweave Continental: Unitarian Universalists for Lesbian, Gay, Bisexual, and Transgender Concerns, with the following mission statement:

> Interweave is a membership organization actively working toward ending oppression based on sexual orientation and gender identity, recognizing that we will not be free until all oppression is a thing of the past. We are a Unitarian Universalist organization and UU Principles guide our work. We value and affirm the lives and experience of Queer people of faith, regardless of their age, race, ethnicity, income level, and ability. By providing and supporting leadership and working in collaboration with other organizations of similar vision, we strive to connect and nurture all Queer individuals, communities, and groups and their allies.

Membership is open to UUs of all sexual orientations and gender identities, and members are encouraged to create local LGBT UU groups and outreach to LGBT communities to promote the religious alternative of Unitarian Universalism.

The UUA endorses the March on Washington for Lesbian, Gay, and Bisexual Equal Rights and Liberation. Thousands of UUs attend the march, and the UUA board adjourns its Boston meeting to reconvene in Washington, DC, and attend as well. Services are held before the march at All Souls Unitarian Church and after it at Sojourner Truth Congregation.

During General Assembly, the UUA board, staff, and GA delegates stage a public protest against North Carolina's "crimes against nature" laws, participating in a candlelight vigil.

The UUA board votes unanimously to make the directorship of the OLGC a full-time position. The office is renamed the Office of Lesbian, Bisexual, and Gay Concerns (OLBGC) to reflect a commitment to the bisexual community.

General Assembly passes a Resolution of Immediate Witness supporting President Clinton's plan to lift the ban on LGB people serving in the military.

The Clinton administration begins the "Don't Ask, Don't Tell" policy, which allows closeted—but not out—LGB people to serve in the military.

1994 General Assembly passes a Resolution of Immediate Witness sponsored by the Youth Caucus urging that sexuality education in public schools be comprehensive, unbiased, up-to-date, and inclusive of all sexual orientations. It also passes a Resolution of Immediate Witness urging UUs to support the Employment Non-Discrimination Act of 1994, which would ban discrimination on the basis of sexual orientation.

The cover of the July/August issue of *UU World* proclaims, "The Welcoming Denomination Faces Down Homophobia." Other articles include "Conversion of a Gay Basher," by Warren Blumenfeld; "Making Love as a Means of Grace," by Rev.

Dr. Rebecca Parker; an article on LGB civil rights by David Reich; and a profile of a gay parent's coming out. The issue includes photos of many UU LGBT folks. Reader response is mixed: the next issue's letters column includes several negative comments along with positive and affirming ones.

There are now 50 recognized Welcoming Congregations (5% of UU congregations).

1995 Rev. Barb Pescan and Rev. Ann Tyndall become the first modern UU same-sex couple to serve together as co-ministers when they are called to the Unitarian Church of Evanston, IL. The milestone is bittersweet, as they first pursued a joint call in 1983 that was blocked by the overt bigotry of congregants.

Mr. Barb Greve is hired into the OLBGC and comes out as transgender/third gender. President John Buehrens, Executive Vice President Kay Montgomery, and other staff are overwhelmingly supportive.

Rev. Dr. Gwendolyn Howard, in her fifth year of serving St. Paul's Universalist Church in Little Falls, NY, comes out as trans to a UUA district official, who advises her to leave her congregation and not tell them why. She does so. Another UUA official later tells her to not expect help from the UUA and to find a new career.

1996 **The US Supreme Court rules in *Romer v. Evans* that legislation banning protection from discrimination based on sexual orientation is unconstitutional.**

The first effective treatment for HIV is introduced, prompting, in 1997, the first decline of the death rate from AIDS in the US since the epidemic began.

President Clinton signs the Defense of Marriage Act, which bans federal recognition of same-sex marriage and allows states to refuse to recognize same-sex marriages performed in another state.

Keith Kron is hired as the director of the OLBGC. The office is renamed the Office of Bisexual, Gay, Lesbian, and Transgender Concerns (OBGLTC) to reflect a commitment to the transgender community.

The UUA board passes a resolution in support of same-sex marriage.

General Assembly passes a Resolution of Immediate Witness supporting the right of same-sex couples to marry. UUA President John Buehrens invites same-sex couples onto the stage in support of the resolution.

Starr King School for the Ministry appoints to the faculty Dr. Ibrahim Farajajé, a Black/multiethnic queer man who eschews labels, and Rev. Yielbonzie Charles Johnson, a Black gay man. Both make major contributions to UU ministerial development and the wider UU movement.

Beacon Press publishes *Transgender Warriors* by Leslie Feinberg, a groundbreaking book that reclaims and recasts transgender history across many centuries and cultures.

1997 General Assembly passes an Action of Immediate Witness urging UUs to support businesses with LGBT nondiscrimination policies, in response to the Southern Baptist Convention's vote to boycott Disney for having such a policy. The same General Assembly engages in a public witness protesting Arizona's laws against sodomy.

The Lambda Ministers Guild, a group of LGB UU ministers that has existed in secret for more than a decade, presents a workshop at UUMA Ministry Days for the first time. It is titled "Gay Marriage, Family Values, and the Struggle for Justice."

OBGLTC provides trainings on transgender issues for the UUA's Ministerial Fellowship Committee, Ministry Department, and Faith in Action Department.

1998 **Matthew Shepard, a young gay man, is tortured and murdered in Laramie, WY. His murder brings nationwide attention to hate crimes against LGBTQIA+ people.**

1999 **Monica Helms designs the transgender pride flag.**

The first Transgender Day of Remembrance is held to memorialize the murders of Rita Hester and Chanelle Pickett, two Black trans women from Massachusetts.

A revised edition of *The Welcoming Congregation Handbook* is released. The new edition is more inclusive of transgender identity, bisexual identity, and the intersections of sexuality with race and ethnicity.

AYS is replaced with Our Whole Lives (OWL), a comprehensive sexuality education program that grows to include curricula for people of different ages throughout the lifespan. OWL is a collaboration between the UUA and the United Church of Christ and continues the groundbreaking tradition of LGBTQIA+ inclusion set by AYS.

General Assembly passes an Action of Immediate Witness urging UUs to work to change the discriminatory policies of the Boy Scouts of America. General Assembly also hosts "The Prom You Never Had," to which it invites local LGBT youth.

2000 **Vermont becomes the first US state to pass a law permitting civil unions between same-sex couples.** The first same-sex civil union ceremony in a UU congregation takes place at First Universalist Parish in Derby Line, VT, officiated by Rev. Jane Dwinell.

25% of UU congregations are recognized Welcoming Congregations. The Liberal Religious Educators Association (LREDA) becomes the first Welcoming Organization.

2001 The UUA Committee on Socially Responsible Investing files a stockholder resolution with Home Depot to prohibit employment discrimination based on sexual orientation. Home Depot adopts the policy.

At General Assembly a same-sex widower of a minister is invited to light the chalice at the Service of the Living Tradition, the first time a same-sex couple is honored in this way.

2002 *The Welcoming Congregation Handbook* is revised to use gender-neutral pronouns throughout.

The first two out transgender UU ministers are called to serve congregations: Rev. Sean Parker Dennison is called to South Valley UU Society, Salt Lake City, UT, as settled minister, and Rev. Laurie J. Auffant is hired by Follen Church Society of Lexington, MA, as minister of religious education.

General Assembly passes an Action of Immediate Witness in support of Quebec's legalization of same-sex civil unions, giving same-sex couples in such unions the same rights as married male-female couples.

2003 **In *Lawrence v. Texas*, the US Supreme Court rules that laws criminalizing sodomy are unconstitutional.**

Rev. Bob Wheatley dies in Cambridge, MA, and the hospital does not initially allow his partner, Kenneth English, to claim his body or make any decisions about its disposition. Rev. Gene Navias later testifies in a Massachusetts state legislature hearing on same-sex marriage, describing English's pain at how he is treated by the hospital.

Crossing Paths: Where Transgender and Religion Meet, a collection of stories and rituals by trans people of faith edited by Mr. Barb Greve, is published by the OBGLTC.

The UUA board appoints Gini von Courter, a lesbian, as interim moderator of the UUA. General Assembly elects her as moderator the following year, a position she holds until 2013.

Dan Savage, journalist and gay activist, is invited to be a featured speaker at General Assembly. His remarks include disparaging and intolerant views toward bisexual and genderqueer people.

Mark Oppenheimer publishes *Knocking on Heaven's Door: American Religion in the Age of Counterculture*, which includes a chapter on Unitarians and gay rights.

Delegates to the General Assembly pass an Action of Immediate Witness on Global HIV/AIDS, urging the UUA to advocate for a stronger U.S. response to the global AIDS crisis.

2004 **Massachusetts becomes the first US state to legalize same-sex marriage without the decision being overturned.** Seven of the fourteen plaintiffs who brought suit against the state identify as UU, including the lead plaintiffs, Hillary and Julie Goodridge. Their marriage license, one of the first, is issued by a UU city clerk, and their wedding is held in Eliot Hall at the UUA's headquarters with UUA President William Sinkford officiating.

After the mayor of New Paltz, NY, is charged with 19 criminal counts after performing 27 same-sex marriages without marriage licenses, Rev. Kay Greenleaf, minister at the UU Fellowship of Poughkeepsie, enlists UU ministers and clergy from other denominations to help marry about a hundred same-sex couples over several months; she and Rev. Dawn Sangrey, a UU colleague, are arrested for this work. The charges are eventually dismissed.

Delegates to General Assembly pass an Action of Immediate Witness opposing the proposed Federal Marriage Amendment.

The UUA launches its President's Freedom to Marry Fund.

Mr. Barb Greve and Rev. Sean Parker Dennison found Transgender Religious Professional Unitarian Universalists Together (TRUUsT). Its mission is to support UU trans religious professionals, help them advocate for each other and their ministries, and transform Unitarian Universalism and our world.

Living the Welcoming Congregation, an online follow-up curriculum to the Welcoming Congregation program, is made available to UU Welcoming Congregations.

2005	**The Parliament of Canada enacts the Civil Marriage Act, which legalizes same-sex marriage in Canada.** 69 out of 74 California UU congregations participate in Standing on the Side of Love Sunday and send 4,000 valentines to Governor Arnold Schwarzenegger in support of marriage equality. The UUA hosts a celebration of the first anniversary of marriage equality in Massachusetts.
2006	Half of UU congregations are recognized Welcoming Congregations.
2007	The UUA board approves a public policy statement advocating equal rights for LGBT people. General Assembly passes Actions of Immediate Witness supporting comprehensive sexuality education legislation, the Employment Non-Discrimination Act (ENDA), and the repeal of "Don't Ask, Don't Tell." It also passes the first resolution that is explicitly trans-related: a Responsive Resolution affirming a commitment to the inherent worth and dignity of every human being, including transgender people, and encouraging UUs to act in accordance with this value and to learn about trans identity. Interweave releases a curriculum on bisexuality, authored by Rev. Ann Schranz, Scott McNeill, Rev. Jane Dwinell, Rev. Amy Zucker Morgenstern, and Dana Dwinell-Yardley.
2008	At Tennessee Valley UU Church of Knoxville, TN, a shooter opens fire in the sanctuary, killing two and wounding seven, in an anti-gay-motivated hate crime. The UUA Committee on Socially Responsible Investing begins filing stockholder resolutions with Walmart to prohibit employment discrimination based on gender identity or expression. After five years of advocacy, Walmart adopts the policy.

2009 **Congress passes the Matthew Shepard and James Byrd, Jr., Hate Crimes Prevention Act.**

At General Assembly, Bruce Knott, executive director of the UU United Nations Office (UU-UNO), reports that the rights of LGBT people were on the agenda of the annual UN Conference on Human Rights for the first time in its 61 years of meetings, with the support and advocacy of the UU-UNO.

General Assembly passes an Action of Immediate Witness resolving to raise awareness among UUs of human rights violations on the basis of sexual orientation or gender identity in Iraq (which was invaded by a US-led coalition in 2003) and urging UUs to pressure the federal government to work with the UN to protect Iraqis targeted in this way.

Standing on the Side of Love (later renamed Side with Love) is launched; it provides a platform for marriage equality efforts and other social justice causes.

The UUA contracts with the Religious Institute to conduct a review and needs assessment of its sexuality-related programs, policies, and advocacy. Recommendations include additional staffing for the OBGLTC, updates to the *Welcoming Congregation Handbook* and other resources, and more programming on trans, bisexual, and intersex issues.

2010 General Assembly passes a Responsive Resolution affirming its commitment to the inherent worth and dignity of every human being, including LGBT people, and urging Unitarian Universalists to work against discrimination against them in employment.

The Office of BGLT Concerns is renamed the Office of LGBT Ministries.

The Ministerial Fellowship Committee adds a requirement that UU ministerial candidates demonstrate competence in sexual health, boundaries, and justice, including LGBTQI issues.

	The US Senate overturns "Don't Ask, Don't Tell," allowing openly LGB people to serve in the military.
2011	General Assembly passes a Responsive Resolution celebrating the passage of marriage equality legislation in New York State. With the recognition of All Souls Church UU, Sioux Falls, SD, the UUA achieves recognized Welcoming Congregations in all 50 US states. Standing on the Side of Love and Church of the Larger Fellowship hold the first denomination-wide online Transgender Day of Remembrance service.
2012	The Office of LGBT Ministries is renamed the Office of Lesbian, Gay, Bisexual, Transgender, and Queer Ministries. Due to UUA departmental restructuring, it is no longer a standalone office with dedicated staff. Genderqueer UUA staff person Alex Kapitan leads a trans 101 webinar for Standing on the Side of Love; the recording becomes the UUA's primary resource on trans identity.
2013	**In *US v. Windsor*, the US Supreme Court declares the Defense of Marriage Act unconstitutional.** General Assembly features gender-neutral bathrooms for the first time, organized by TRUUsT, 10 years after the General Assembly youth and young adult caucuses passed statements asking for gender-neutral bathrooms. Interweave releases a curriculum on transgender welcome, authored by Johnny Blazes and Julia Terry.

2014	General Assembly approves a change to the UUA bylaws that adds an article on inclusion, which pledges to replace barriers caused by systems of power, privilege, and oppression with ever-widening circles of solidarity and mutual respect. It also adds gender identity and gender expression to the bylaws' nondiscrimination clause. General Assembly also passes an Action of Immediate Witness declaring support for a Quaker project to help LGBTQ people in Uganda flee persecution there.
2015	**In *Obergefell v. Hodges*, the US Supreme Court guarantees same-sex couples the right to marry, legalizing same-sex marriage in the US.** At General Assembly, same-sex couples are invited up to the stage to celebrate marriage equality (recreating the first invitation in 1996). Rev. Sean Parker Dennison gives the prestigious Berry Street Essay.
2016	**North Carolina bans people from using public bathrooms that correspond with their identity rather than the sex on their birth certificate. Although it is eventually partly repealed, the law signals the beginning of a new wave of political and cultural attacks on trans people.** **A mass shooting at Pulse, a gay nightclub in Orlando, FL, kills 49 and wounds 53.** General Assembly passes an Action of Immediate Witness calling on UUs to condemn anti-trans legislation and work to protect and support trans and gender-nonconforming people. TRUUsT holds its first membership retreat; 15 trans UU religious professionals attend. 75% of UU congregations are recognized Welcoming Congregations.

2017	The UUA board appoints Mr. Barb Greve and Elandria Williams, both of whom are genderqueer, as interim co-moderators of the UUA. The following year General Assembly elects Greve (and Williams's board term continues); the two serve as co-moderators until 2020.
2018	The UU Retired Ministers and Partners Association (UURMaPA) launches the UU Rainbow History Project. TRUUsT and the UUA jointly conduct a survey of trans UUs that finds that 72 percent do not feel fully included in their congregations. Nearly half of respondents report regularly experiencing trans-related marginalization in UU spaces; higher levels are reported by those who are financially insecure, people of color, nonbinary people, and/or disabled people. The Transforming Hearts Collective releases *Transgender Inclusion in Congregations*, a program for UU congregations created by Rev. Mykal Slack and Alex Kapitan.
2019	**Far-right US politicians begin campaigning on the topic of trans girls in sports.** UURMaPA holds two conferences focused on the Rainbow History Project, to mark the 50th anniversary of the Stonewall Rebellion. The UUA's LGBTQ Ministries office launches an initiative for congregations to renew their Welcoming Congregation designation annually. Five trans ministers are called to new UU congregations as settled ministers, an unprecedented number. Only one of these settlements will last more than four years. *UU World* publishes its first feature story about trans, nonbinary, and intersex people. The article, which contains inaccuracies and normalizes insensitive treatment of trans people, is very poorly received by trans UUs and sparks debate. The following issue of *UU World* includes an apology and features content by trans UUs.

At General Assembly Rev. Todd Eklof releases the self-published book *The Gadfly Papers*, which kicks off a wave of racist and anti-trans public rhetoric within Unitarian Universalism.

2020 **Idaho becomes the first US state to pass a law banning trans women and girls from female sports teams in public schools.**

In *Bostock v. Clayton County*, the US Supreme Court rules that Title VII prohibits discrimination on the basis of gender identity or sexual orientation.

The UUA joins amicus briefs in *Bostock* and also *Masterpiece Cakeshop v. Colorado Civil Rights Commission*, a US Supreme Court case arguing for religious exemption to discriminate on the basis of sexual orientation.

2021 **Alabama becomes the first US state to pass a law banning gender-affirming health care for trans minors.**

General Assembly passes an Action of Immediate Witness urging UUs to condemn anti-trans legislation; increase the material inclusion of trans, nonbinary, and intersex UUs; and affirm that "living one's identity, in terms of gender identity/expression, sex characteristics, and affectional/sexual orientation, is part of our free exercise of religion."

2022 **Increasingly repressive anti-LGBTQIA+ bills are proposed in many US states, including bills that seek to ban all mention of LGBTQIA+ topics in schools and bills that create religious exemptions for discrimination.**

The UUA authors an amicus brief in a court case challenging Alabama's ban on gender-affirming health care for trans minors.

The Pink Haven Coalition is formed, initially as a partnership between the UUA, Unitarian Universalist Service Committee, and a trans-led organization, to help trans people in crisis due to the increasing anti-trans movement.

2023	**The number of anti-LGBTQIA+ (mostly anti-trans) bills proposed in US states and Congress skyrockets, particularly bans on gender-affirming health care for trans minors.** General Assembly elects Rev. Dr. Sofía Betancourt, a queer Afro-Latine cis woman, as its first out queer president. She has been previously appointed by the UUA board as interim co-president for a three-month term in 2017. General Assembly also passes an Action of Immediate Witness calling on UUs to work for health equity, including gender-affirming health care.
2024	General Assembly passes, with 92% of the vote, a Business Resolution that declares that full affirmation and celebration of transgender, nonbinary, intersex, and gender diverse people is a fundamental obligation revealed by UU Principles and values and that our covenant binds UUs to honor, defend, and celebrate the spectrum of gender identity. *Authentic Selves: Celebrating Trans and Nonbinary People and Their Families* (Skinner House Books) is chosen as the 2024–2025 UUA Common Read. **Donald Trump wins election for a second (non-consecutive) term as US president, creating fear for LGBTQIA+ and other people who have been targeted by the policies and actions of his first administration.** UUA Executive Vice President Carey McDonald comes out publicly as nonbinary transgender, the most senior out transgender person to ever serve on UUA staff.
2025	**As the second Trump administration begins, assaults on the rights of LGBTQIA+ people accelerate. In his first week in office, Trump issues three anti-trans executive orders, seeking to regulate sex as binary, erase legal recognition of trans people, ban trans people from the military, and ban all gender-affirming care for people under age 19.**

On the first day of General Assembly, the UUA condemns the US Supreme Court ruling in *US v. Skrmetti*, which upholds Tennessee's ban on gender-affirming care for minors. A special session is added to the agenda to address the implications, led by LGBTQIA+ human rights advocate Sam Ames and UUA General Counsel Adrienne Walker.

The Ware Lecture at General Assembly is delivered by Imara Jones, award-winning journalist and trans rights activist.

General Assembly passes an Action of Immediate Witness calling on UU congregations to take action to practice solidarity with global LGBTIQ movements in the midst of massive politically motivated funding cuts.

The UUA joins an amicus brief urging the US Supreme Court to uphold Colorado's ban on conversion therapy in *Chiles v. Salazar*.

President Sofía Betancourt joins ten other heads of diverse religious traditions in issuing a landmark interfaith statement proclaiming that transgender, intersex, and nonbinary people are worthy of love, support, and protection. She is the lead author.

Coming Home

Rev. Virginia Wolf

As a child in the 1940s and '50s, I was a tomboy who wanted to be a real boy. As a teenager, I had crushes on my history teacher, Miss McGrew, and a classmate, Karen. My teacher married during the year that I gave her my devotion. Karen married between her junior and senior years of high school. These early years of adolescence confused me. My crushes on Miss McGrew and then Karen were intense and obsessive. I kept a scrapbook about my teacher and went to her room every night after school to talk and to help her, if I could. She filled up my emotional life, but when she married, I withdrew. My relationship with Karen was even more powerful than the one with Miss McGrew. I wanted to be with her all the time, or to be on the phone talking to her. At some point, it became very obvious that Karen was boy-crazy. We drove around looking for boys, sometimes stopping to chat and flirt. Eventually, she met her future husband, and our friendship began to wane. I was devastated.

I was uncomfortable with boys, but I got the picture. I learned that crushes on girls were likely to end in suffering, and that I needed a boyfriend to be acceptable in my high school. Wayne, my friend in the Civil Air Patrol, was the answer. He was good-looking enough, respectable, a year older, and willing. But women friends held my attention. Donna, Ann, Wykeemah, and Marietta were my inner circle.

I entered the University of Kansas and moved into Watkins Scholarship Hall in 1957, still amazingly naïve. One woman, Sylvia, was the talk of our class. She had a great figure, striking clothes, a worldly attitude, and apparent contempt for many of the women. For some reason I did not understand, she started to hang out with me.

At first Sylvia and I were just good friends, studying together and pulling one escapade after another. We drank and smoked (to excess), went to parties where drugs were readily available (although I never tried any), and skipped classes, sneaked out of the hall, and drove to Kansas City to black night clubs where we were the only white faces. During the summer after our freshman year, I longed to be with her and persuaded my parents to let me drive the fifty miles between our hometowns. She, in turn, visited me. When I asked her many years later what I meant to her, she said I was her teddy bear or her security blanket. I, on the other hand, never felt safe during the years we were together.

Once again I had a crush, but I no more understood what was happening to me than I had in the past. I first heard about lesbians during my sophomore year when I met Shirley, and Sylvia and she began a relationship. During these years, Sylvia also slept with several men. Eventually, I persuaded her to become my lover. I was head over heels in love with her and tried to be with her all the time. While it was clear she cared for me and liked to be with me, I knew all too well that she was more important to me than I was to her. Many evenings and nights she was elsewhere, and I drank. I hated the way I felt. One semester my grades slid so low that I was in danger of losing my scholarship. I knew I was harming myself, and yet I couldn't stop. Looking back, I can see that I was frightened. I had no idea what was going to happen to me. I could see no way that Sylvia and I could be together in the future. I was nearly certain that she would not want to be with me. I wasn't sure I wanted to live a gay lifestyle. I had little idea what one might be. I was sure that most people would reject me if my lesbian identity were known. I dated men in an effort to prove to myself that I was not a lesbian. I even got engaged to my high school boyfriend. I floundered, searching for a life independent of Sylvia.

My junior year was just as intense as my sophomore one—eventually even more so. Again my grades slipped, and I was saved only by my cumulative record. But the big event was Sylvia's roommate catching us making love in their room. We were sent to the dean of women's office and threatened with expulsion unless we stayed away from each other and entered therapy.

This was in 1959. Homosexuality was still listed as a mental illness in the *Diagnostic and Statistical Manual of Mental Disorders*, as it had been since 1952 and was until 1973. Most lesbian, gay, bisexual, and transgender people were hiding. Bars, the only place lesbians had to meet, had to pay off the police and were still occasionally raided. In the summer of 1962, a friend from the university and I drove across the country to a Girl Scout camp near San Francisco, and I was in a San Francisco lesbian bar when the police arrived. My friend and I escaped down the halls of adjoining buildings and thus avoided being arrested. I am glad I was with someone who knew the score.

In the sixties, some bars in some cities started refusing to pay off the police. There were many seeds of gay activism, but they would not begin to flower until the Stonewall Riots in 1969.

After we were caught, Sylvia and I did not see each other much, except at a distance or in the company of other people. This does not mean that I did not want to be alone with her. The second semester of my junior year was tough. I was taking over twenty credits and had changed majors. I was drinking less, studying hard, and going to classes. But I was seeing a therapist who was a jerk. He saw my wearing pants to his sessions as defiance of him and of therapy and kicked me out. I was devastated. I hadn't consciously worn pants to be defiant, but I was so unsure of myself that I wondered if he'd been right.

Luckily, I found another therapist with whom I could relate and who supported me in my efforts to sort out my childhood and my college years. I saw him once a week until I graduated. He recommended that I enter psychoanalysis at the Menninger Clinic in Topeka, Kansas, on a scholarship program. I set about finding a teaching job near Topeka.

In order to be accepted for analysis at Menninger's, I had to take a full day of tests and my parents had to come up for conversations with the doctors, which made them very uncomfortable. In the end I was accepted because, I was told, I revealed sufficient intelligence and creativity to make it likely that I would make a significant contribution to society. Shortly thereafter, I began with Dr. Ammon at Menninger's, going five times a week, for $25 a session.

I was in analysis to end my attraction to women. Much of this involved my reclaiming my love for my father. I am thankful for this experience, thankful I was able to stop hating my dad for being a drunk. I am also grateful for the self-confidence I acquired as a result of Dr. Ammon's support. For the first time in years, I was not afraid of sleeping in the dark.

Challenged to change my appearance, I lost weight, got contacts, had my hair styled, and bought new clothes. I quit drinking. Dr. Ammon told me that there was no such thing as a lesbian, that lesbian experience was at most a phase of development into full womanhood. I didn't quite believe him, but I wanted to. I wanted to be fixed. I didn't want the shame and degradation and hiding involved in being a lesbian. Two years after I started graduate school, Dr. Ammon declared me cured enough and ended analysis.

Shortly thereafter, I began dating John. Dr. Ammon had warned me not to get involved with anyone for a year, but I did it anyway. This was a magical time for me, even though something was always nagging at the back of my mind. John and I talked and laughed, went to interesting places, and hung out with a group of clever graduate students. He was planning on going to Honduras to set up a philosophy department, and it was exciting to talk about.

Then I got pregnant. I didn't want an abortion. John and I were only in the dating phase of a relationship, and neither of us was really sure what to do, but gradually we decided to get married and go to Honduras together. It wasn't an easy decision, and after six years (two in Honduras and four back in Kansas) and two babies (1966 and 1971) we separated. I was angry with him all the time for not doing housework and childcare. I had no time to study for my preliminary exams for my PhD, and he was having affairs. After three years of separation, I filed for divorce.

Never once during those nine years did I consciously look at a woman as a potential lover. My earlier lesbian experience was buried deeply inside me. But the end of this relationship made me feel inadequate, as if I wasn't enough of a woman to make it work. I felt like a failure. Now I wonder how much those feelings were due to shame about my relationship with Sylvia.

The year 1975 was a turning point in my life—or, more precisely, a whole series of turning points. My divorce became final. Carol Schumacher, who was to become my wife, moved into my basement, exchanging childcare and housework for room and board. I had joined a consciousness raising (CR) group, and we began to talk about lesbianism. Carol came out to me, and when her lover broke up with her, she spent hours talking to me about the relationship. Then Marnie in my CR group asked me out, and I started talking to Carol about that. The result of all that talking about other women was that Carol and I fell in love and began a relationship that has now lasted for nearly fifty years. It was so clear that this relationship was what my body, mind, and heart wanted. I felt as if I had come home.

But it took me a long time to get over my internalized homophobia. My college experience had left deep scars, whereas Carol, who is fourteen years younger than I, was much more at ease with her sexual orientation. My parents believed homosexuality was a sin, as my brother and sister may still. They were loving when I finally came out to them, after ten or so years of bringing Carol with me on every visit. They knew she was a good person, good for me and for the children. Still, they did not approve and did not wish to talk about it. I did talk about it, and they listened, although they never said a word. Carol's family, on the other hand, embraced both her and me wholeheartedly, although sometimes Carol's mom was delightful in her confusion about what to get me for Christmas. One year I would get what she gave to the sons and sons-in-law, and the next what she gave to the daughters and daughters-in-law.

Another difference between us was that Carol was familiar with lesbian culture and I was not. She took me to concerts where there were lesbian performers and bookstores where there were numerous novels and works of nonfiction written about and by lesbians. We played lesbian music at home and read as fast as we could, and went to lectures about lesbian and gay people. Most important, there were lesbian groups and friends. Now living in Eau Claire, Wisconsin, we started a group in our home and met friends of friends, discovering and developing a wide network of lesbians from the Twin Cities to Tomah. We went to dances, pig roasts, movie nights, and ball games. We talked and talked about what it meant to be a lesbian.

I came out slowly, over a period of twenty years. I was afraid that if I was too open about being a lesbian, John might try to take the children away, that I might lose my job, my friends, and the respect of my students. But even though I didn't go around announcing that I was a lesbian, Carol and I always went everywhere together as a couple, sometimes with our children. Of course, many people recognized that we were lesbians. I can think of two occasions upon which this became dramatically obvious. When our congregation was beginning the process of calling a minister, a woman came out from denominational headquarters to inquire as to our willingness to call a lesbian or a gay man, and one of the elders of the church responded, "Why wouldn't we, when for years we have had strong lesbian lay leadership?" The second example was less pleasant. I was running for chair of the English Department at the University of Wisconsin–Stout, and I began to hear from my friends that a smear campaign was being mounted against me. People were claiming that because I was lesbian, I hated men. Both of these experiences, and many others as well, make me think that I might have been better off being more open. But I was afraid and had a lot to lose. I did what I could do.

Eventually, I became courageous enough: the culture became more positive, and I had less to lose. There is no doubt in my mind that secrets are toxic. As Carol and I became more out, we were much happier. I remember delivering my first professional paper about sexual orientation in 1987, "The Gay Family in Literature for Young People." My anxiety was sky-high. But everyone who had been my friend still was, and they respected me more for taking this risk. At church, people welcomed Carol and me as a couple. We had a (nonlegal) wedding in 1990, on our fifteenth anniversary, and the church was packed. In 1992, I published my study of the lesbian author Louise Fitzhugh (creator of *Harriet the Spy*), and in my discussion of Fitzhugh I also came out myself, and again people responded positively. I met two of my closest friends because they heard that I was a lesbian and approached me. When I worked as the special assistant to the university chancellor, Carol and I were included in university social events as a couple.

When I attended the UUA's Midwest Leadership School in the summer of 1990, I took another step. A rather large number of gay and lesbian people were there, and there was some tension around gay issues. We organized into a formal group to talk about being UU and being gay, which increased the tension with the people who were not in the group. I experienced myself as a leader both in the discussion group and among those not in it, and I sought to make peace. I was completely out and felt very vulnerable, but I discovered that my sexual orientation didn't determine how people looked at me—or how I looked at myself.

My becoming a minister had a lot to do with my sexual orientation. Unitarian Universalism has a long history of supporting LGBT people. In 1977, the Eau Claire congregation welcomed us as a family. They nurtured our talents and our children. In this congregation, I felt completely at home, welcomed, and accepted as a lesbian.

I felt the same way at United Theological Seminary of the Twin Cities, where I enrolled in 1993. When I first visited, there were materials on the bulletin boards that were gay-friendly. I was out to all my professors and classmates and met other gay people who were also. There was a group for us, the Mariposa Alliance. When I wrote, I discussed my lesbian identity and the way it influenced me to think as I did.

Only once did I encounter opposition, and that from a student with whom I worked on a group presentation about the family and the church. My part of the project was about the gay family, and this student asked that I present "both sides" of the topic! I was shocked, but I responded that I didn't know that there were two sides. It became clear that he wanted me to offer arguments both for and against the gay family, and I refused. Fortunately, the rest of my group took my side.

My professors were much more than merely accepting. Some of them expressed gratitude for my openness and participation. One of them recommended me to *Open Hands,* a journal for those seeking to be in ministry with LGBT people, which was looking for someone to write about being a gay seminarian; my article was published in 1994. I planned a conference for gay seminarians and helped lead a workshop on the gay family.

When I was called to my home church in 1999, I was no longer attempting to hide that I was a lesbian. Of course, everyone who knew me was fully aware that Carol was my partner. The Search Committee wanted to know how open I would be. I said "very open" and explained that things would not change for us until the straight world began to question its assumption that everyone was heterosexual. In order for people to recognize me as a lesbian, I had to come out over and over again, although I hope that a time will come when sexual minorities won't have to do this.

So in sermons, I mentioned my partner. I gave sermons about homosexuality. I stood up in public for same-sex marriage; indeed, Carol and I applied for a marriage license sometime in the late 1990s, fully knowing that we would be refused. We arranged for Fair Wisconsin, a statewide organization working for gay rights, to meet in the church. In 2005–2006, we canvassed against a proposed amendment to the Wisconsin constitution that would ban same-sex marriage, and when it passed, we took part in an ACLU lawsuit to compel the state to establish domestic partnerships for same-sex couples. When that suit was won, in 2009, Carol and I became the first couple in Eau Claire County to apply for one. The state appealed the case, but it was finally settled in our favor in 2012.

Even before that case was settled, the ACLU decided to challenge the constitutional ban on same-sex marriage in Wisconsin and asked us to be the lead plaintiffs in the new suit (*Wolf v. Walker*, 2014). We already had plans to marry in Minnesota, where same-sex marriage had been legalized in 2013, so that we would at least have federal marriage benefits. Then we learned that Wisconsin's marriage evasion law threatened us with fines and even jail time if we married in another state and came back to Wisconsin, where our marriage was illegal. Thinking the publicity might be good for the cause, we went ahead with our plan, and the ACLU's suit also demanded that we be protected from harm under the marriage evasion law. Once again we won, the state appealed, and we won again. Same-sex marriage became legal in Wisconsin in September of 2014. Other states decided to take their case to the Supreme Court, which decided in our favor on June 26, 2015.

It's been an amazing whirlwind of a journey. The press has interviewed us countless times. Our application for domestic partnership was a front-page story, and our participation in the multiple lawsuits was also covered. Our chances at marriage seemed hopeless in 2006, when Wisconsin passed the constitutional amendment. Then in 2013, the Supreme Court ruled that section 3 of the so-called "Defense of Marriage Act" was unconstitutional and that the federal government could not discriminate against married lesbian and gay couples for the purposes of determining federal benefits and protections. The floodgates were open as state after state, including Minnesota and then Wisconsin, established same-sex marriage, until four years later it became the law of the land. Only four years! I never would have believed it, but I am deeply happy and satisfied to have arrived here on my journey toward acceptance of my being gay.

Butterflies

Rev. Dr. Sandra Szelag

Since third grade, I have been aware of being different in my attractions. In college, I engaged in several secretive lesbian relationships. During those closeted times of the early 1960s, though, I kept denying my sexual preference and tried to disprove it to myself. I remember going to the bookstore in my college town and buying some books on homosexuality, telling the clerk they were assigned for a class. I hid them from my roommates. All those books said I was mentally ill.

My young adulthood as a closeted gay woman unfolded in the context of protest movements and social upheaval: the fights for civil rights, peace in and withdrawal from Vietnam, women's rights, and gay rights. Although the Voting Rights Act was passed in 1965, obstacles were thrown up to prevent Black Americans from registering to vote, especially in the South. That spring Rev. Dr. Martin Luther King Jr. led six hundred people in what became the first of three attempts to stage a march of protest from Selma to Montgomery, Alabama. Many were injured, jailed, tear-gassed, and beaten by Alabama state troopers on the day that became known as Bloody Sunday. I remember watching the events unfold on television with horror and disbelief. I was a high school English teacher at an all-white school in the Chicago suburbs, and when Rev. Dr. King was killed in 1968, the PA system interrupted my advanced English class to announce his death and call for a moment of silence. Several students stood up, marched around the room, and thrust their right arms into the air in a Nazi salute.

The National Organization of Women (NOW) was founded in 1966 to fight many forms of discrimination against women. In 1970, the fiftieth anniversary of women gaining the vote in America, women staged "Women's Strikes for Equality" across the nation. In 1971, after much internal controversy, a NOW resolution finally recognized lesbian rights as a legitimate concern of feminism. And in 1973, the Supreme Court rendered its decision in *Roe v. Wade*, affirming a right to abortion as the law of the land.

During the 1968 Democratic National Convention in Chicago, protest groups showed up in large numbers to demonstrate. Mayor Daley promised "law and order," and in the name of law and order, Chicago police used tear gas on protestors, shoved them through plate glass windows, and beat them as they sprawled on the broken glass. The violence was later deemed a "police riot"; friends and I had to scramble to escape. All of it was broadcast live on TV as the anti-war protesters chanted, "The whole world is watching." One hundred protesters were treated for injuries and six hundred were arrested.

Many things have changed since then for LGBTQ people, and some sadly have not. Here's some of how it used to be:

- When I was young, the words *gay* and *lesbian* could not be printed in a newspaper, as they were considered indecent and offensive. *Queer* was an extremely derogatory word.
- Before 1962, sodomy was a felony in every state, punishable by a lengthy term of imprisonment and/or hard labor.
- The American Psychiatric Association considered homosexuality a mental illness until 1973; the American Psychiatric Association did so until 1975. Shock therapy and even lobotomies were sometimes performed as "cures."
- Until 1982, there were no state laws against discrimination based on sexual orientation. Discrimination in employment,

housing, education, and public accommodations was legal and common.

- Between 1973 and 1993, more than two-thirds of the public considered homosexuality to be "always wrong," and only about 20 percent said it was "never" or "only sometimes" wrong. Today, 76 percent of the public supports LGBTQ rights.
- There was no such thing as a state-recognized civil union or domestic partnership until 1999, and no state-recognized same-sex marriage until 2004.

In May of 1970, a friend invited me to attend a service at her church, the First Unitarian Church of Chicago in Hyde Park. I had been raised a Catholic but left the faith in 1961. I had no interest in church or religion, but she insisted and I finally agreed. It was the first Sunday after the Ohio National Guard had shot unarmed students protesting the Vietnam War at Kent State University on May 4, wounding nine and killing four. Reverend Jack Mendelsohn, the minister in Chicago, canceled the regular planned service and instead conducted a memorial service for the students who died.

As I sat there, listening to the inspiring music of the Chicago Choir and the International Children's Choir, I felt moved by Rev. Mendelsohn's words, which affirmed my own values and concerns. As I looked around, I saw a culturally and racially integrated congregation. The safety and support that I felt so deeply that morning enveloped me and brought me home to myself. I became active in the church and in the denomination. My life changed dramatically. That summer, I quit my teaching job rather than remain closeted or be fired. I finally came out. Soon, I would also take up the cause of gay rights.

The 1969 Stonewall riots in New York City kicked off the gay rights movement, but I never said "I am gay," to myself or anyone else, until 1970. I certainly never said, "I am gay and I am proud." All that was about to change.

On June 28, 1970, the one-year anniversary of those riots, thousands of people marched through the streets of Manhattan from the Stonewall Inn to Central Park in what was then called "Christopher Street Liberation Day," one of America's first Pride parades. The parade's official chant was "Say it loud: Gay is proud," a rallying cry for people to stop hiding in closets of shame.

I joined a radical Unitarian Universalist group called the Fellowship for Renewal that same year. The group held weekend retreats and was active in support of the UU Black Caucus and, later, the UU Gay Caucus. Some members of the FFR formed a commune, which I joined in 1971. We all worked part-time, so we could devote much more energy to social activism.

In 1971, I went to Washington, DC, for my first Unitarian Universalist General Assembly. It was there that I joined the newly formed UU Gay Caucus, founded by Richard Nash. It was composed mostly of men; there was one other woman besides me. She eventually shared with me that her lover had been forced by her parents to undergo a lobotomy when they found out that she was gay.

I learned that GA had passed a resolution the previous year to immediately "end all discrimination against homosexuals and bisexuals" both within the UUA's churches and fellowships and within the larger society. But there was growing controversy about that position, which meant that there was much more work ahead of us.

During that time, in the interest of dispelling stereotypes and myths; educating congregations; creating spaces of freedom for closeted gays and lesbians in their own religious communities; and encouraging supportive non-gay clergy and laypeople to come forward, several of us formed the Chicago Gay Caucus. We developed a worship service, which went on the road to Chicago-area Unitarian

Universalist churches. Many of us participated, so of course, since it was the seventies, we all piled into a VW van—a rather unreliable one, I might add. In the van, we bonded and prayed, Unitarian style of course, that we would arrive on time to our destination and safely back home.

We called our service "Lost and Found: A Celebration of Gay Identity." The opening words to the service were always "We can feel that shared identity coming through—an identity of a people hidden so long from each other, but finding ourselves now, and staying together." Readings consisted of everything from Sappho to Walt Whitman to poetry challenging the Biblical story of Sodom and Gomorrah. Personal sharing made up a powerful portion of the service. I provided a closing statement that depicted the difficult process of coming out as an act of faith, using the symbol of a butterfly that tentatively emerges from the darkness of a cocoon, uncertain of finding light. I extended the symbol to point out the need for unity and diversity to emerge in our Unitarian Universalist community—a closing that I expanded and included in a 1973 sermon I had the privilege of delivering in Boston. At the end of the service, the congregation sang "Morning Has Broken," and those who felt that they could fully welcome sexual minorities into their church were invited to come forward and stand with the group as a recording of activist Madeline Davis's speech from the steps of the New York state capitol was used as a benediction. We also sometimes played her "Stonewall Nation," the first gay liberation song. After the coffee hour, we traditionally gathered at a Chicago gay restaurant for a champagne brunch, which we invited anyone from the congregation to join. Brunch always included some people who had come out to their congregation at the end of the service.

The larger, national UU Gay Caucus continued its work at General Assemblies. We gave speeches, staffed an information booth, held educational workshops, and networked with other groups within the denomination that were supportive. We even distributed buttons that said things like "Homophobia is a social disease." My favorite was one we gave to people who said they didn't see a problem in our denomination: "How dare you presume I'm straight?" We gave them that button and challenged them to wear it during GA and come back to report the reactions they encountered. After the sweeping resolution in 1970, the UUA launched About Your Sexuality, a new sexuality education program that taught positive attitudes toward homosexuality and bisexuality, as the resolution urged. That too became controversial.

The concept of an Office of Gay Affairs (OGA) at the UUA, with gay staff, began to take shape as the next step. It would help the organization and all Unitarian Universalists move beyond myths, stereotypes, and discrimination. A resolution to create such an office was hotly debated at the 1973 GA in Toronto. Tension filled the chamber. One who adamantly opposed the office was Donald Harrington, the prominent and admired minister of the large, influential Community Church of New York. After the resolution finally passed, we claimed victory and went home to celebrate. He went home and delivered to his congregation an infamous anti-gay sermon, twenty pages long and widely circulated. He made the same arguments that Christian fundamentalists and evangelicals still do. However, unlike Christians, who quote the Bible and call us sinners, he relied on quotes from the most condemnatory figures in the fields of psychiatry and psychology, who argued many outlandish opinions, including that there was "no such thing as a healthy homosexual." He feared that our youth would be inculcated, that families and society would be destroyed by the "dogma" just passed by the UUA GA. Fortunately, some other ministers, like Robert S. Lehman and David R. Weissbard, delivered and published supportive sermons.

The Office of Gay Affairs still had to be approved by the Board of Trustees and funded. The board was scheduled to meet four short months after GA, on October 26, 1974. Henry Weimhoff and I were given the privilege of becoming co-coordinators of the Chicago Gay Caucus. We all agreed it was time to have both a woman and a man as leaders. Along with Clark House and David Steege, Henry and I became the strategy task force of the national caucus and strategized ways to convince the board to vote in favor of establishing the Office. This was a formidable challenge, since Bob West, the UUA president, was opposed to it and Donald Harrington's arguments were taken seriously by many. The opposition to us was intensifying. Meanwhile, other members of the UU Gay Caucus formed task forces to explore access to funding and created an outline for the form and structure of the office.

Part one of the strategy was a conference of the Gay Caucus held in Boston the weekend of October 5 to gain local support, to coordinate the work of the task forces, and to finalize the strategy for the October 26 board meeting. With the help of Margaret Herrick and Phyllis Schmidt of the Arlington Street Women's Caucus, the Gay Caucus was able to secure the use of the Arlington Street Church for the conference. On Saturday, we met with a group of staff members from UUA headquarters. Among them, only Hugo Holleroth seemed firmly in support. Bob West did not attend because he was going to Europe and didn't have time. We learned that many at UUA headquarters were offended by the word *gay*. We told them that objecting to the word *gay* in the office's name and proposing to call it the Office of Homosexual Affairs instead was insulting and only proved how badly it was needed. David and I also objected to the fact that *UU World* only published negative letters about the proposed office. The magazine's editor, Doris Pullen, was at the meeting, and she agreed to print positive letters, which she did.

On Sunday morning, Rev. Leslie Cronin, assistant minister of the Arlington Street Church, led a service centered around the presence of the Gay Caucus, in which I was to speak. In my mind, I was giving a "talk," but the order of service used the word *sermon.* In addition, Rev. Cronin was the very first female UU minister I had ever met. The neurons in my brain began to fire: *Oh, a woman can be a minister.*

Although I had spoken in many UU churches before, this service was nerve-wracking. The pulpit was extremely high, and I was afraid I would fall as I climbed the many stairs; how embarrassing that would be! I did not fall. Yet I was uncomfortable being high above the people seated below. For the last portion of my talk, I took the microphone, walked down the stairs, and finished on the same level as the congregation.

Just as my first time attending the First Unitarian Church of Chicago in 1970 changed my life, this 1973 experience in Boston did too. On my flight back to Chicago, I realized that I, a woman, could become a minister and that much of what I had been doing in those three-plus years was the work of ministry. By the fall of 1974, I was a student at Meadville Lombard Theological School in Chicago, which meant that I was also enrolled in classes toward a master's degree at the University of Chicago.

But for now the task in front of me and the Caucus was to return to Boston in less than three weeks for the October 26 board meeting, and to convince the board to approve the Office of Gay Affairs. Henry, David, and I flew back to Boston. Edna Griffith, a board member from Iowa, happened to be on the same plane, and during the flight we were able to gain her support. The night before the meeting, we held an open house at the Copley Hotel for board members, giving them an opportunity to meet us informally. They welcomed the opportunity to ask questions, express concerns, discuss issues, and gather more information.

The board meeting took place on Friday afternoon, October 26. Henry and I were designated as spokespersons. President West introduced the issue of the office by presenting three options, all of which we considered untenable. One suggested that the Gay Caucus become an affiliate and conduct its own programs. Another one proposed that the office be called the UUA Homosexual Office, have no funding from the denomination, and be restricted only to educational work, forbidden to advocate or "promote" homosexuality.

As Henry and I listened to the discussion that followed, we saw clearly the value of the previous night's open house. Board members who had attended argued against all the options Bob West presented. They also adamantly rejected the use of the word *homosexual* in the name of the office. Then I presented the Caucus's statement in support of the proposed office, which outlined our arguments.

More discussion ensued, and Henry and I answered questions. Toward the end, objections were raised to the word *affairs* in the office's name, which for some evoked a sexual connotation. The Caucus had heard this concern already and was prepared; we informed the board that we would gladly accept the name "Office of Gay Concerns." After two hours of deliberation, a simple hand vote was taken and the board approved the office's creation by a vote of eighteen to eight. All the Caucus members who were in Boston celebrated this victory before heading home to prepare for the next fight: to force the UUA to fund the newly approved office.

For the UUA, this was one small step further on the road to embracing its gay and lesbian members. For me, it was a huge step on my road to ministry. I went on to complete my studies at Meadville Lombard, becoming a Reverend Doctor; to intern at the Unitarian Universalist Church of Tucson; and, in 1977, to be ordained at the First Unitarian Universalist Church of Chicago, where this new chapter of my life had begun seven years before. I continued to be out of the closet, working to continue educating people and advancing the causes the Caucus had taken up in the 1970s.

I used the symbol of the butterfly emerging from the darkness of a cocoon in both my closing words for the worship services offered by the Chicago Gay Caucus and in my Arlington Street sermon. The darkness of the cocoon represents the closet, the place where we hide in self-hate and fear and consume the unpalatable myths about us that society feeds us. Our emergence into the light is an act of faith, for there is nothing to inform our choice. We don't know the beauty of ourselves as butterflies or the thrill of flying.

If we were all merely individual butterflies, our story could end here. However, we are not only individuals, but individuals in community. We participate in a community of Unitarian Universalists and also in the larger society; we do not and cannot exist in isolation. And morning may have broken for us as individuals, as we emerge from our closet cocoons, but it has not yet done so for us as individuals in community.

Our communal metamorphosis, our joint breakthrough to the morning light, is a struggle toward unity in diversity, which cannot be established unless we encounter each other and ourselves with openness and trust, humbling ourselves before the mysteries of our shared existence. If we do not reach consensus on issues, we have only diversity, which by itself is alienating and self-seeking. If we reach consensus without confronting our differences, our unity is only conformity, which is empty and meaningless.

The breaking of this communal morning is the real underlying theme and meaning of my story. In the words of James Baldwin, "The moment we cease to hold onto each other, the moment we break faith with one another, the sea engulfs us and the light goes."

My records of gay and lesbian activism in the Unitarian Universalist movement go back to 1970, tracing the history from the first anti-discrimination resolution passed at that year's General Assembly and covering the formation of the UU Gay Caucus and the successful fight for an Office of Gay Concerns to be established, funded, and maintained at the UUA headquarters in Boston.

What is not in the files, of course, is the intensity of emotion that charged these events with fire, urgency, and determination. Also absent from the files are the warm, talented, dedicated gay and lesbian friends and comrades with whom I stood arm in arm. We grew and endured together through the insults, the frustrations, the disappointments, the strategizing, the laughter and support, the struggles to defeat homophobia through education, and the joyful tears of sweet victories, and we built community in UU congregations through creative celebrations of worship. I invoke their presence by listing their names: Elgin Blair (also known as the Great Monarch Butterfly of the North), Henry Weimhoff, Clark House, Joe Norton, Ann Bennett, David Steege, Julie Lee, Ernie Potvin, Margaret Herrick, Hal Lawson, Mara Shelby, Skip Ward, John Kyper, John Smith, Floyd Hof, Kirk Perrow III, Wayne Moore, Richard Nash, Frank Robertson. Trailblazers, one and all.

Times Have Changed!

Dr. Helen Bishop

When my wife Susan and I began looking for a Unitarian Universalist congregation in the early 1980s, we were looking for a religious education program for our five children. We'd already tried several Protestant denominations, but all of them made it clear there was no room for us. I'd been to a UU congregation when I was in college and thought one would be worth a look. We lived in southern California then, and we decided to try out a UU congregation on the coast. They were friendly and, not recognizing us as a couple, said we must be sort of like Kate and Allie, the title characters of a sitcom about two (straight) women who move in together after they both get divorced. That interpretation was fine with us then, so we stayed for several years. But when the cover story no longer suited us, they made it clear we were no longer welcome. So we headed for a much larger congregation in San Diego, and we didn't come out to them. Our children were welcomed there; they became active in Liberal Religious Youth and formed lasting relationships and friendships.

The congregation sponsored potlucks for people who wanted to talk about issues affecting LGBTQI+ people in San Diego. We were terrified that someone would find out we were lesbians raising children. Since we didn't receive child support, it was up to us to earn the money it took to raise five children, and we were afraid we would lose our jobs, the house we were buying, and custody of the children. We used to come in at separate doors for the potlucks. We sat separately, brought two potluck dishes, and acted as if we were friends, not partners. The ministers, Revs. Tom and Carolyn Owen-Towle, attended the potlucks regularly, and often entered into the discussions. Still, LGBTQI+ people remained mostly closeted, although some of the men were active in the gay community in the downtown San Diego area where most of them lived, called Hillcrest.

At that time, the congregation was divided about how LGBTQI+ people should be treated. The ministers were supportive, and most people thought we should be welcomed, but there were some who openly said that "these people" were an abomination, people with a mental disease. The UUA staff claimed that none of them was "like that." The Pacific Southwest District had never offered a workshop about LGBTQI+ people. Although it was the 1980s, the opinions and attitudes of the McCarthy era and the homophobia of J. Edgar Hoover still persisted. Through it all, the ministers continued to encourage Unitarian Universalists to be more open and welcoming. The congregation's policies gradually changed to reflect new understandings about LGBTQI+ lives.

I had become active in religious education by that time, although it was clear that the religious education community, the UUA, and most congregations would only be comfortable with us if we remained closeted. We got involved with the UU organization that became Interweave, founding a local chapter as well as attending annual conferences. At that time, no openly LGBTQI+ ministerial candidate had been ordained, and no openly LGBTQI+ religious educator was part of the Liberal Religious Educators Association (LREDA).

I was serving on the Interweave board and was also part of the Common Vision Planning Committee. In 1987, we decided it was time to find out how Unitarian Universalists felt about openly openly lesbian, gay, and bisexual leaders, including ministers and religious educators. We decided to publish a survey in *UU World.* The surveys came back to me, and I prepared a report for the UUA board, showing that Unitarian Universalists were quite divided on this subject. About half the respondents thought UU congregations could be served well by LGB leaders. About half wrote that LGB people had a mental illness that could be treated, or that they should undergo conversion programs to "cure" them. Some respondents described plans to assault or kill us.

We submitted the report to the board in January 1989, and the board decided that the Association needed to maintain staffing focused on LGB issues. They increased the hours of the director of the Office of Lesbian and Gay Concerns, Rev. Jay Deacon, and requested a program that ended up being called Welcoming Congregation. I wrote a curriculum for our congregation that served as an introduction to the concepts of the Welcoming Congregation program. Meanwhile, the surveys were stored in boxes in our attic. No one had thought about where they might be archived. Eventually, some of the responses were included as a leader resource in a Tapestry of Faith curriculum called "Resistance and Transformation" and can still be found on the UUA website.

By then I had written my dissertation and received my doctorate in organizational leadership from the University of San Diego. The UUA was advertising for someone to become the district executive of the Central Midwest District; district executives answered to the UUA and also to their district boards. I thought I had the qualifications they were looking for and applied for the job. I interviewed in Chicago and in Boston and was offered the position. I'm not ordained, I am lesbian, and I have a permanent disability. I thought I'd be on a steep learning curve, and I was correct. Nonetheless, I accepted the offer, and Susan and I packed up our house and moved to Chicago. The boxes of surveys went with us.

The Welcoming Congregation program was well received by many UU congregations. The director of the Office of Lesbian and Gay

Concerns helped Interweave assist UU congregations with learning to welcome LGBTQ members, ministers, and religious educators. Congregations were often still reluctant to call LGBTQ ministers, so we did a lot of comforting at Interweave convocations. Overall, however, there was greater acceptance for openly LGBTQ people.

After eight years, my tenure as district executive came to an end. I accepted a position at The Mountain, a camp and conference center in western North Carolina, where I worked on leadership training for Unitarian Universalists. Susan and I ended up moving again, this time to northern California, where we were able to go because the job at The Mountain involved distance education. We couldn't bring those boxes of surveys with us, since they took up quite a bit of space. I contacted places I thought would be willing to archive them, but no one was willing to take them. We decided we needed to dispose of them, but we were concerned about doing so in a way that might let someone opposed to LGBTQI+ people find them and use the information in them to harm people. We ended up driving around Chicago, putting the boxes in various recycling containers. Today, I'm guessing that I could find an archive that would want to preserve them.

Susan and I were legally married in North Carolina in 2014. We were the subjects of a lead article in our local newspaper, and no one seemed to have a problem with it. Unitarian Universalists understand intersectionality better now and acknowledge the roles of race, class, ability, and other aspects of identity that can lead to marginalization. Times have changed, as have the options for living openly as LGBTQI+ people. Still, the loss of those surveys remains on my mind. I wish we could move more quickly, for the sake of people of color, people with disabilities, working-class people, and others, especially those who are trans. We need to keep working as Unitarian Universalists for greater justice in these key areas.

You Can't Preach Here! You Can't Marry Here!

Eric Schuman

In writing this essay, I ask the reader to understand its context. I'm writing from my memory of events occurring up to thirty-eight years ago. I've consulted my records, but neither they nor my own memories are infallible. Be assured I've done the best I can to recount events accurately. For any errors, I accept full responsibility.

Just before Christmas 1982, a brief article in *UU World* struck me as odd. It announced that a resolution would be voted on at the 1983 General Assembly to affirm the right of UU clergy to perform same-sex unions in our congregations, without interference from any trustees or fellow clergy.

I wondered what the need could be for a resolution like this. That some UU clergy around the country were performing same-sex unions was no secret. Such things happened regularly. I hadn't heard of ministers facing any repercussions for performing them, so why was a GA resolution needed?

Thinking about who might be well enough connected to know the answer, I phoned Rev. Frank Robertson, minister of religious education at All Souls Church in Washington, DC. Widely respected and well known in our movement, Frank was an out gay man who served on the UUA Board of Trustees. I was living in Topeka, Kansas, and we'd last seen one another earlier that year at General Assembly in Maine.

"How are you, Frank?" I asked. His reply took me by surprise. He explained that it had been the worst year of his ministry and that he was suffering from severe job-related stress caused by conflict with his senior minister, Rev. David Eaton, and the All Souls board. David and I knew each other from when I had been a member of All Souls in 1969 and 1970.

Frank had performed a same-sex union at the church for two African American women, and an article describing the event, with an accompanying photo of the couple in the All Souls sanctuary, had been published in *Jet Magazine*, a periodical read by many of the congregation's Black members. A number of laypeople who objected to the service approached Rev. Eaton and brought a resolution to the Board of trustees that prohibited same-sex unions from being performed in the sanctuary and forbade all clergy except the senior minister from participating in them. The resolution passed with unequivocal support from Rev. Eaton, who was probably the most prominent African American minister in our denomination at the time.

Frank was worried that he would be terminated for his role in bringing attention to the church because of his support of same-sex unions. Indeed, he was gone within the year, although I don't know if he was forced to resign or terminated. The person I was calling to ask why the GA resolution was needed was the very minister whose victimization by a homophobic congregation made the need for it obvious.

I was deeply disappointed and angered by what I learned from Frank. I gave considerable thought to what I might say to David if I saw him at GA in Vancouver the following year. When I did encounter him there, I told him he had missed a critical opportunity to support a different marginalized group of people: gay and lesbian folks like me. (I hadn't previously come out to him.) He became quite defensive, arguing that Black members of the congregation had wanted the resolution and that he was obliged to support them.

He told me I didn't understand Black folks, to which I replied that I recognized homophobia when I saw it and I hoped that he would recognize it someday as well. I suggested that as a result of the policy passed by his board they might want to consider purchasing a bus to be stationed in the All Souls parking lot, and instead of conducting same-sex services of union in the sanctuary, they could do them in the back of the bus. He wasn't amused. That was the last time I would see David Eaton.

The resolution proposed at the 1983 General Assembly did not pass. That GA was to prove critical in the history of Unitarian Universalists for Lesbian and Gay Concerns (UULGC). After the resolution's failure, the group demanded justice from the UUA for its lesbian and gay members. For most of the group, same-sex union ceremonies were an absolute requirement: nothing less than a strongly worded resolution endorsing them would satisfy our need for justice.

Even so, I saw a more compelling issue at the time. Two young, openly gay ministers, Barbara Pescan and Ann Tyndall, were aspiring to become co-ministers at Community Church in New York City, one of our urban churches that had been most successful in racially integrating its congregation. It was also known as one of the most progressive congregations in the city, championing many local peace and justice issues. During candidating week, an open meeting of the congregation was called where more than one member said they were "appalled, horrified, and disgusted" that lesbians could possibly become their ministers. One member recalled that "speaker after speaker built up the hatred and bigotry, calling Ann and Barbara 'scum' and 'mutants.'" The vote to reject them was 55 to 38.

One openly gay man, Doug Strong, had been called to a pulpit in Maine, but no openly gay woman had ever been called by a UU congregation at that time. This discrimination was a sign of the homophobia that was ubiquitous in our congregations. Rev. Charles

Gaines, the UUA's director of ministerial settlement, told me in 1988 that a survey by his department showed 37 percent of respondents would object to a gay or lesbian ministerial candidate (and 3 percent would object to a Black one). Several gay clergy recounted stories of being rejected by a congregation when their professional packet mentioned their sexual orientation, and being hired by a different one after removing it. The wider denomination was aware of the problem: a 1980 General Assembly resolution called "Ministerial Employment Opportunities" had called on our churches, the UU Ministers Association, and the Department of Ministerial and Congregational Services to assist gay, lesbian, and bisexual religious leaders with settlement. Kay Montgomery, the UUA's executive vice president from 1985 to 2013, said to me in the late 1980s that homophobia in settlement went "to the heart of who we are," perhaps more than any other issue facing the UUA, and that how we handled this "profound moral dilemma" would say a great deal about how seriously we chose to live our professed values, purposes, and principles. I agreed completely.

After the resolution failed in 1983, I argued that UULGC should devote its energy in the coming year to combating homophobia in ministerial settlement. But I did not prevail. The overwhelming majority of members preferred a year-long action directed at affirming same-sex unions. After the motion for this passed, the next step was to find a member willing to do the work of coordinating a binational campaign (since Canadian congregations were then members of the UUA) to get the resolution passed once and for all. At that time, I was serving as president of the Prairie Star District, comprising eight states and two Canadian provinces, and UULGC members hoped that I might be able to wield enough influence to make it happen. Although my heart was with the issue of discrimination in hiring, I was willing to take on the task, because UULGC had deemed it our first priority.

By the mid-1980s, UULGC had become a significant presence in the denomination. Nevertheless, lesbians and gay men were routinely left out of decision-making at the highest levels. At the 1983 General Assembly, Rev. John Buehrens, who was at that time a UUA board member, announced the appointment of the Task Force on Social Responsibility to thoroughly evaluate denominational efforts for social justice and social change, which would include racial justice, peace, and the Office of Lesbian and Gay Concerns—but when he announced the members he had appointed, none was an openly gay man or lesbian. I added the matter to the UULGC agenda, and we drafted a demand to Rev. Buehrens and the UUA board that an openly gay man or lesbian be appointed. We even nominated two prominent UULGC members and included their credentials. His response? The board appointed a closeted minister not included in our list of recommendations. This incident reminded me of the old saying "If you don't have a seat at the table, it's probably because you're on the menu."

I had no experience coordinating a national political campaign, so I consulted one of my most knowledgeable and experienced friends: Dru Cummins, the UUA trustee representing the Prairie Star District and first vice moderator of General Assembly. Dru's position was that as long as the Services of Union resolution was categorized as a general resolution, it was unlikely to pass because it was competing with issues of global and national significance. The key to passage was to change the wording so that instead of merely expressing support for same-sex unions, it required UUA staff to expend time and money, thus qualifying it as a business resolution. I wrote the language Dru suggested, she reviewed it and made editorial suggestions, and then the campaign began. The newly worded business resolution not only supported freedom of the pulpit for clergy to perform same-sex unions without interference from their congregation but also requested that the UUA develop and distribute materials that would explain such services to laypeople and help clergy prepare and perform them.

We sent the resolution to all UUA districts for their endorsement, asking them to submit it for inclusion on the agenda of the 1984 General Assembly in Columbus, Ohio. We encountered little difficulty in obtaining the required number of district endorsements, but there were significant challenges from UUA legal staff and the General Assembly Planning Committee, which repeatedly rejected our requests to submit it as a business resolution. We persisted at every possible venue, including the UUA board, which advised UULGC to once again change the wording slightly. The board then submitted the resolution for consideration at GA itself, by unanimous agreement of its members.

UULGC members and supportive friends from all over the US and Canada helped to promote the resolution at the congregational and district levels. I coordinated strategy for the floor fight at General Assembly and recruited key people from around the continent to speak in Columbus. When the issue came to the floor for discussion, it was clear we'd done our homework. The opposition seemed less organized and eloquent. On the other hand, at least no one suggested that passage of this resolution would lead to further resolutions promoting bestiality, as Rev. Donald Harrington had in response to a gay-affirming resolution in the 1970s.

We had no idea what the outcome would be, but the Services of Union resolution passed by an overwhelming majority. We didn't know that reporters from the Associated Press would cover the vote; articles on it appeared the next day in newspapers all over the country, including the *New York Times*. Other than the Metropolitan Community Church (a predominantly gay Protestant denomination) the Unitarian Universalist Association had become the first religious body in the world to endorse same-sex unions!

The UUA also elected a new president at the 1984 GA. Sandra (Sandy) Caron, the UUA moderator, had announced her candidacy more than a year earlier, and I had gotten to know her through my work as district president. An attorney who regulated banking in New York State, she was intellectually sharp, assertive, and personable. She solicited my support, and I gave it willingly. Many months later, Rev. William F. (Bill) Schulz announced his candidacy. He had begun working for the UUA as director of the Office of Social Responsibility and became executive vice president in 1979, during the term of Rev. Eugene Pickett. I admired Bill's accomplishments, and I had worked with him to plan a twenty-fifth anniversary observance of the *Brown v. Board of Education* Supreme Court decision in 1979, which was co-sponsored by the UUA and my home congregation of Topeka, Kansas.

At a dinner Sandy and I had together in 1983, I told her how concerned I was about Barbara Pescan's and Ann Tyndall's experience with Community Church in New York. I told her that, if she was elected, I hoped one of her first priorities would be to work against homophobia in hiring at the administrative and congregational levels and among the regional ministerial settlement representatives (MSRs) who were a key part of the hiring process at that time; they represented the UUA to congregations seeking ministers.

In response, she told me she had risen to the top of the New York banking regulation industry, an almost entirely male world. She said she had faced sexism at every level, and that if she could break through those ceilings on her own, so could lesbian ministers. She would offer no support to out-of-the-closet lesbians seeking pulpits. I was appalled and uncertain how to proceed.

Shortly before a district presidents' meeting in Boston, Bill Schulz phoned me to ask for a meeting in his office. To my surprise, he solicited my support for his candidacy, and I told him that as much as I admired him and would support him were he elected president, I had already pledged to support Sandy.

"What would it take to change your mind?" he asked. I asked if he knew about what had happened to Ann and Barbara at Community Church, and he said that he did and was shocked by the congregation's homophobia.

"What can you do about the issue of discrimination against gay and lesbian ministers seeking pulpits?" I asked.

"When I'm elected, I'll do everything possible to change the settlement process so that this never happens again."

"But your responsibilities as executive vice president include the ministerial settlement process. What are you going to do now?" I asked.

"What would you suggest?" he replied.

In 1982, a fledgling UU gay and lesbian group in Minneapolis had asked the Prairie Star District for a grant of $234 to help with promotional expenses. I spoke on their behalf, but the motion died for lack of a second. I was so angry that I considered resigning. Instead, I used district funds to arrange for a workshop on homophobia in hiring practices in my own district. It was led by Rev. Morris Floyd, a United Methodist minister working as the director of a lesbian and gay community service center. His facilitation skills were brilliant, and he earned uniform praise in evaluations from our board. So I suggested to Bill that he have Morris provide similar training to the UUA board and the MSRs.

Bill did win the presidency, and the whole way in which the UUA helped congregations call settled ministers radically changed. As soon as they began the process, congregations seeking ministers were educated about the UUA's commitment to fairness in hiring and the denomination's history of support for gay and lesbian rights (six relevant resolutions had been passed at General Assemblies between

1970 and 1980), as well as its support for women, people of color, and people with disabilities. In 1989, a program called Beyond Categorical Thinking began bringing them teams of experts on fairness in hiring. The UUA board and staff seriously considered not assisting congregations in search that would not equally consider women, LGBT candidates, candidates of color, or disabled candidates, but the "stick" approach was rejected in favor of the "carrot" of persuasion and education.

Some of our UULGC members were deeply disappointed that the UUA had not elected Sandy, who would have been its first female and first lay president. My strong support of Bill's candidacy and my criticism of Sandy for her opposition to changing the ministerial settlement process lost me a few friends. Although I was hurt by this, there was no question in my mind that my efforts were worth the price I had paid and the long hours I had spent working for change in the UUA. I've never regretted my decision, and I'm proud of the small role I was privileged to play in making the UUA more just to LGBT ministers and same-sex couples who want to marry.

Before There Were Heroes

Rev. Kimberley Debus

As a young queer cis woman in the seventies and eighties, I was already the beneficiary of those who came before. In my teens, I was introduced to the music of Cris Williamson, Meg Christian, and Holly Near. I discovered Rita Mae Brown's *Rubyfruit Jungle* and the poetry of Adrienne Rich. As the eighties became the nineties, I cheered when Ellen came out on national television and when Melissa Etheridge and k.d. lang came out through their music and concerts.

These were my heroes. Women a half generation before me, showing me it was possible to be queer. I wore my lesbian identity proudly, being part of a Lesbian Avengers group, belonging to a lesbian chorus, organizing Pride marches and events for women-only spaces. I had dozens of older sisters cheering me on, grateful for my youth and energy.

And something was still missing.

I suppose I always knew I was bisexual; my crushes were on both boys and girls (we still thought gender was binary then) and I had sexual experiences with both. But after some disastrous relationships with men, I fell in love with a woman and decided that was it. I was a lesbian. The impulse to lean into the sisterhood was strong and comforting, and it helped me forge an identity and build a place I thought I could call home.

Yet the crushes on men continued, and I kept them like a dirty secret. I remember telling the first partner I thought I could trust with this, and while Trish accepted it joyfully, she issued a stern warning: "Do not tell anyone about this."

Trish's words reinforced my secrecy, even as we worked tirelessly under the LGBT banner. We were so proud to have fought for the inclusion of a trans woman into our midst. We publicly maintained that "it doesn't matter who you love, love is love." Yet for all of our rhetoric, it was clear that my supposedly LGBT community did not believe the B. I grew to understand the B as meaning "not really gay" or "can't make up their minds" or "horndog" or "we want a threesome."

After Trish died in 1998, I gained comfort not from my gay and lesbian friends, but from my straight male friends. They seemed to hear the pain in my heart—especially one friend, Mark. Mark's comfort was inviting, and my relationship with him did turn romantic for a while. And that was fine. My mistake was telling my lesbian friends, who branded me a traitor to the sisterhood, called me a "hasbian," and ostracized me from the community I had loved and served in for years.

I had nowhere to turn. No heroes to look to for inspiration or comfort. I had no community left, and I decided that since I was not attracted to women at the moment, my lesbian days were over. I was . . . well, I didn't know what I was. When I started dating again, I dated men—some of whom thought my past relationships with women were a turn-on, and some of whom tried to convince me I was straight now.

And something was still missing.

What was missing, as it turns out, was not a hero to look up to, or a community to define me, but a simple way to define myself. It was the simple definition provided by Robin Ochs in her 2014 essay "Bisexuality 101":

> Bisexuals are people who acknowledge in themselves the potential to be attracted—romantically and/or sexually—to

> people of more than one sex and/or gender, not necessarily at the same time, not necessarily in the same way, and not necessarily to the same degree.

I was bisexual all along and didn't know I could claim the B. I didn't know because there were no bisexual heroes for me as a young bisexual person. I didn't know because the community drew the circles too tightly. I didn't know because there were no out bisexuals in the media to look to.

I am now an out-loud-and-proud bisexual. I am bi in my relationships, bi in my attitude, bi in the pulpit.

And yes, being bi in the pulpit can be a challenge. I learned from my years serving a congregation that even the most enlightened congregant tends to identify a person's sexuality by the person they date. When I spoke about Trish's death in one service, the congregation assumed I was lesbian. When I mentioned a man I had had a relationship with in a different service, I got a series of very carefully worded questions from people who didn't want to pry but were absolutely confused by my use of different pronouns. And once I was explicit about being bisexual, explicit biphobia reared its ugly head, with people now asking questions about my "real" preference, suggesting that I was confused or conflicted, and once even advising me to get therapy to "answer the question once and for all." And although I now have plenty of bisexual colleagues, all of us often find this ground difficult to travel. We seek support and models to help the people we serve—and us ourselves—understand that nothing about sexuality is cut and dried, but instead it is much more nuanced, more varied, and infinitely more delightful.

We carry on. We find our way. We name our identities and challenge the status quo. We ask for nuance and curiosity. And . . . we figure out how to model this for those who come after us.

The philosopher Soren Kierkegaard said that life is lived forward but understood backward. Here at age sixty, I look back on this journey and see that in fact, I was the hero I had long sought. I blazed my own path, held my own romantic and often wounded heart, and affirm to myself and the world that there will be better days when we embrace our truths.

An Inconvenient Family

Rev. Aija Simpson-Newbury

A note on queerspawn and queer identity: *It is important to me, and to the many queerspawn friends I've had over the years, that we do not identify as allies of the queer community. Whatever our respective gender and sexual identities, and we do run the gamut, we all identify as* members *of the queer community. To be the child of a queer person is to inhabit a very specific and unavoidable role in our communities. We are the bogeypeople that conservatives mean when they clutch their pearls and cry "What about the children?" We are the ones who have to prove that our parents are capable of raising us and the ones who have to bend over backward to explain who is connected to whom and what specific acts were involved in our conception. And yes, people have asked. Often. We have had to edit our forms and educate our teachers. To be the child of LGBTQ+ people is to be in the fight whether you like it or not.*

The thing about allies is that if the going gets tough, they can leave. People are often wary of allies for just this reason. Will they stay when it gets hard? Do they really care as much as we do? So no, I'm not an ally, no matter who I date or long for or build my life with. I'm part of this team too. I had a queer conception, and I plan to have a super queer funeral.

"We just got married! Surprise!" That's how my mom started the phone call. It was Valentine's Day, 2004. Then she told me to turn on CNN, as though this was a perfectly normal request, and promptly hung up the phone; she had other people to call. In a bit of a daze, I tuned on the television, flipped around channels, and was suddenly greeted with the announcement that Gavin Newsom, then mayor of San Francisco, had declared gay marriage to be legal. And so my mother was able to marry my other mother, her partner of twenty-four years.

After the fact, my moms realized they weren't really quickie courthouse wedding types, and they went about planning a huge church wedding at my home congregation, the First Unitarian Universalist Church of Berkeley. Or perhaps I should say that my mother delegated to other people the task of planning their church wedding, and by other people, I mean *me*.

My home congregation was large by Unitarian Universalist standards, with more than four hundred members, and I promise, they all turned out to help. One congregant rebuilt the candle stands that were used on Christmas Eve so that we could have a candle-lit wedding at dusk. Other people brought in Christmas lights that transformed the foyer and the social hall into a twinkling party room. And then, the night of the ceremony, they all showed up.

When you are the adult child of two people getting married, it is not entirely clear what role you are supposed to play in the proceedings. I was too old to be the flower girl. I couldn't be either of their best women, because who would I choose? I could read a poem, but that seemed sort of . . . small for such a grand occasion. After much conversation, it was decided that I would open the ceremony, welcome the guests, and introduce the occasion.

Standing before all the guests that evening, welcoming my religious community into one of the most joyful events in the life of my family, and having them magnify that joy with their presence was one of the most powerful moments of my entire life. I knew I was exactly where I was supposed to be, and in that moment, I truly opted into Unitarian Universalism. This was my church, this was my home.

I was not new to Unitarian Universalism. At that point in my life, I had been attending that same church on and off for more than twenty years. But it was in that moment that I truly decided, that I committed to this religious identity in a way I never could have before. In that moment of such full immersion in what it means to be part of a community, what it really means to share our joys and sorrows with each other, I got it. I opted in.

This congregation, which was so willing to stand with my parents that day, stayed with them. In the depressing, draining, and ultimately doomed fight to defeat Proposition 8, the 2008 ballot initiative that made same-sex marriage once again illegal in California, my church took a stand. Our ministers supported their non-UU colleagues who faced censure and even dismissal over their decision to bless same-sex marriages. We ran a phone bank, marched in protests, and when I was jumping around like a fool on the overpass at 5 AM the day of the election, trying to get passersby to see my "NO on Prop 8" poster, I was flanked on either side by members of my church.

Do you know how important that was to me? When so many religious institutions tell their members over and over again that your family is wrong, that homosexuality is sinful? The message that "God hates gays" was pretty well accepted as truth. But my church told a different truth. You are not different from us. You are loved and cherished, by us and by God. It makes all the difference in the world.

But my home congregation did not always know how to proclaim this truth. When my parents first arrived in 1984, my church was not anti-gay, but it was ambivalent on the issue. They operated under an implicit "Don't Ask, Don't Tell" policy. There had been the occasional gay man who attended. There was a closeted gay staff member whom everyone loved and no one spoke openly about. Our family was something new, and we presented a consistent, inconvenient challenge.

The church did not quite know what to do with this odd family who showed up and, weirdly, kept showing up. Did the religious education curriculum need to be changed? Did the language that was used when talking about committed relationships need to be altered? Were they supposed to fly a Pride flag next to the one for the United Nations at the front of the sanctuary? So many new questions, all seemingly small, but they kept coming. How were they to deal with this new territory, the changing nature of what it meant to be a family within the larger church community? What do you do with people who refuse to be invisible?

The congregation faltered. But we were lucky, primarily because we didn't have to figure out how to do this on our own. When Unitarian Universalists speak of "our church," we often mean our individual congregations. The legacy of congregational polity, under which individual, autonomous churches make their way on their own, is strong with us. But it is not all that we are. We are also the larger church: we are individual congregations, but we are also the Unitarian Universalist Association. And the UUA had a head start on my congregation in figuring out how to do this.

- In 1970, thirty-five years before my parents stood before our congregation and declared their love for each other, General Assembly passed a resolution encouraging congregations to "bring an end to all discrimination against homosexuals." A call that seems self-evident to us now was then revolutionary.
- In 1973, GA passed a resolution to open an Office of Gay Concerns within the UUA. *And they funded it two years later.*
- In 1984, GA passed a resolution encouraging congregations to perform same-sex union ceremonies.

- In 1993, eighteen years before the government caught up, the UUA encouraged the military to stop discriminating against openly gay soldiers.
- And in 1996, eight years before my parents' first, legal wedding, GA called for legal same-sex unions.

This is just a sampling of the ways in which our faith tradition chose to lean into inclusion. We weren't always perfect, but we consistently chose radical love. And we followed with other changes. New, progressive religious education curricula that included a wide range of sexual orientations and family structures. The Welcoming Congregation program, which helps churches to learn how to open their doors and their hearts to gay people, lesbians, bisexuals, transgender people, and folks with identities we haven't even learned the names of yet. But we will.

It is to this Unitarian Universalist Association that my home congregation turned. My congregation learned to be proud of the diversity of its families. These days, my wife and I are a nonissue, just one of the many lesbian and gay couples with kids in the family ministry and religious education programs, not to mention the wide variety of other people who call our church home. My congregation learned to tell itself, and the community around it, that all were equal in their faith, and my denomination brings that same message to the world.

We speak often of Unitarian Universalism as a chosen faith. Usually when we use this language, we are referring to people who have chosen this faith instead of another religion, the religion into which they were born or in which they were raised. But I think that we all have to choose our religion, every day. Every time you come to church, you are choosing your religion. Every time you fill out your pledge form, you are choosing your religion. Every time you go to a committee meeting or a church social, you are choosing your religion. And those of us who were born into this religion have to choose too. At some point, you have to decide: Are you in or are you out? I chose in.

I chose Unitarian Universalism because it chose me. It chose my family and my friends and (some of) the people in my community. This has been one of the great successes of our faith. But we have yet to figure out how to choose *all* of our people. People show up at our churches every day and, like my family once was, are greeted with confusion and with good intentions that still cause harm. Trans people, poor people, people of color, people with different abilities and different accents. There are too many people whom we haven't yet welcomed into our circle of radical love.

I have been both deeply healed and profoundly disappointed by our faith. When we are part of a community, when we take it seriously and ask that it take us seriously in return, that is what happens. When I choose our faith, I choose to take responsibility for it. For me that means working to make sure that everyone who walks through our doors feels as welcome and seen and needed as my family came to be. Like our faith, I have faltered in this more often than I have succeeded. But I look back on our history and I see the ways our community can change, because I see the ways it already has. I see a community that has struggled to expand its definition of *we*. May we never stop.

A Queer Co-Ministry Love Story

Rev. Wendy Bartel and Rev. Lynn Gardner

Rev. Lynn Gardner (they/she) and Rev. Wendy Bartel (name, not pronouns) are co-ministers. This is written in the style of their shared sermons—changing voices, offering perspectives, and weaving music throughout, including by using song titles as headings.

Wake, Now, My Senses

Wendy: For many years, I was an active out queer and genderqueer person in my home congregation in San Diego. I began attending the First Unitarian Universalist Church of San Diego in the fall of 1990. Revs. Carolyn and Tom Owen-Towle were my ministers until they retired. Their faith and trust allowed me to flourish in a religious community when hardly any other religions were tolerating, let alone welcoming, young people like me. I served on committees and task forces, led adult religious education classes, organized and participated in large events, etc. For more than a decade, I was encouraged to go to seminary, especially after leading worship or leading the children's choir. But I couldn't afford it and I liked my life in San Diego, where I had a relatively successful music therapy business, friends, and church.

Then three things happened.

First, the 2000 presidential election results were, to me, unfavorable, and the radical right was getting louder, stronger, and more hateful.

Second, I looked at the websites for Meadville Lombard Theological School and Starr King School for the Ministry and as I read the words of welcome and reviewed the application process, felt a sense of something like "oh dang, I might need to seriously consider this."

And third, the Owen-Towles retired, and during the candidating week for the new minister, the congregation sang #298 "Wake, Now, My Senses." I suddenly and deeply knew as the fifth verse began—"Wake, now, my vision of ministry clear"—that it really was time to answer the call to ministry. But how?

At a picnic celebrating the newly called minister, three different people approached me and said that if I wanted to go to seminary, they would create a scholarship to help offset some of the enormous expense. So I applied to seminary, and then for UUA scholarships as well. I was very active in the UU Musicians Network (now the Association for Unitarian Universalist Music Ministries), and when I shared the news that I was going to Starr King to continue to deepen my antiracism and antioppression work, two folks from Oregon told me to be on the lookout for someone named Lynn. They thought we might hit it off.

When I moved to Berkeley in 2005 to start at Starr King, my partner and I decided to stay together long-distance for the first year. Our relationship was loving and also complicated. Over time, it became clear to me that this was not going to work out, even as I still love this wonderful person.

I marveled quietly, in my introverted and shy way, at how much professors and other students knew about history, the(*)logies, popular culture, how to study, while I figured out how to use my laptop and flip phone(!) in seminary life while navigating student loans, off-campus housing, and managing an impossible course load of reading.

It became clear that friends would be crucial to a fruitful ministry.

Lynn: It was the first day of orientation at Starr King School for the Ministry in the fall of 2005. The incoming class of twenty-six students found seats in the Fireplace Room, and I looked around with nervous anticipation and excitement. We had introduced ourselves to one another via email, and some of us had already met in the process of moving to the East Bay, which most of us had needed to do in order to attend seminary.

These were the people who I would learn with and from, the people who would become my colleagues and, hopefully, my friends. I knew that sitting in that room were people who would become both dear to me and necessary for my survival in ministry. I wondered about the conversations, connections, challenges, and adventures that lay ahead.

I had been encouraged by Rev. Gretchen Woods and the music director at my home congregation in Corvallis, Oregon, to connect with someone named Wendy, who they knew from the UU Musicians Network. Wendy and I met during that orientation.

In our first semester we were in a preaching class together, where each student offered two sermons. I had loved being part of worship in Corvallis and weaving the various elements of the service together was important to me. And I remember the day that Wendy offered a sermon. Before starting, Wendy handed out an order of service, saying, "I think of worship holistically, and these are the elements that would go with this sermon."

I was moved by Wendy's words and message and felt energized by Wendy's style and creativity. During the break, I was in the small kitchen at the same time as Wendy and enthusiastically said something like "Oh, my gosh, I just loved your sermon! It would be so fun to work with you!" Wendy looked surprised and a bit overwhelmed by my excitement.

Over the next few months, as we attended classes, programs, and chapel services, we became good friends. We knew that ministry wasn't easy and that having the support of friends and colleagues was important. One day, we promised to be radically honest with one another and to risk saying hard things with care.

While our seminary lives overlapped in many ways, our personal lives were quite different. Wendy had a partner who lived in San Diego. I had a fourteen-year-old daughter (Meghan), lived with my husband of twenty years, and worked two part-time jobs. My husband, an alcoholic, had begun drinking quite heavily again. I attended Al-Anon and was beginning to address my codependent thoughts and behaviors. Couples therapy helped me set boundaries, and to eventually choose to end the marriage.

In 2003, when Meghan was in seventh grade, she had attended OWL (Our Whole Lives). I was grateful for the body- and sex-positive curriculum and the fantastic facilitators. During that year, she and I had a number of important conversations. I told her that I identified as queer and that I experienced attraction to people of various genders.

As the divorce was finalized, I reminded her of that conversation. "OK," she shrugged. Then, months later, during her sophomore year, we sat on the couch and I told her that I was, in fact, interested in someone, and that it was actually someone who she already knew and loved. It was hard at first. "Now I have to think of you differently," she said. After a day of taking in this information and what it meant for each of us, she was ready to talk more, and to welcome Wendy as my partner.

As our relationship deepened, we grew as a family, too. I became a better parent, and Wendy and Meghan developed their own relationship.

Something to Talk About

Wendy: We started dating (which for the most part meant studying on the same couch) for a few weeks before we shared the news with the wider Starr King community. When we did, we were a little surprised that most of the reactions were along the lines of "It's about time!"

As our relationship deepened, we decided that we were drawn to co-ministry. To find out if that might work, we set up some opportunities for our ministerial formation. We took some classes together. We co-led a few chapel services at Starr King. We served on the Chapel Committee together. We preached together in about ten congregations in our district over a few months.

In a world that promotes individualism and independence, we thrived working collaboratively, sharing these experiences of serving together, our gifts weaving interdependently. We learned so much about congregational dynamics, about assumptions that lay folks make about the nature of worship, and about ourselves and our own processes of creating and writing.

Then we went looking for a unit of clinical pastoral education (CPE) to do together. There were a few programs that seemed like a good fit, but the CPE supervisors that we contacted were not interested in having a couple in the same program.

Eventually, we found a program and a CPE supervisor who was intrigued with the idea. We were intentionally open about our relationship with the other participants in our cohort and asked them to tell us directly if any of our relationship dynamics negatively impacted them.

Despite valiant efforts by the staff, poverty and structural racism were pervasive at the hospital. In those ten weeks of summer 2007, we learned a lot about pastoral care. We learned to listen with open hearts and to pray, when asked, in the way of another's the(*)logical beliefs. It was deep formational work.

Better Together

Lynn: We were invited to participate in Clergy Couples, a group for partnered ministers of whom at least one is UU. Some couples serve in a parish, some in community ministries, and some are retired. About fifteen at the time were co-ministry teams. With all the differences, there was also the common experience of having a partner who was also called to serve. When the group met for their annual gathering just prior to Ministry Days, we were warmly welcomed. We met more of the co-ministry teams, heard some of their stories, and learned the many different ways they worked together.

We were a bit of an anomaly. At the time, there weren't other queer couples serving together, nor were there co-ministry teams graduating seminary together. We were given helpful advice about being in search, serving together, and tending to our personal relationship. We heard how often congregants projected parent type issues onto those co-ministers.

We continue to apply much of what we learned from these beloved colleagues.

Then it was time to apply to internships. Our daughter would be a senior in high school, and we all wanted her to stay in the same school. Thankfully, both of us were accepted into local internships. Wendy's site included a lead minister and assistant minister. Mine included a co-ministry couple and a minister of religious education.

We are eternally grateful for our internship supervisors and the ways they supported our individual learning and our desire to be a co-ministry team, including scheduling each of us to co-lead worship in the other's internship site. And the assistant minister and the minister of religious education are also a clergy couple who were of course, part of our learning!

Free in You

Wendy: We finished our third year of coursework and began preparing for internship. That spring, on May 15, 2008, the California Supreme Court determined that same-sex couples had the right to legally marry in the state; the decision went into effect on June 17. We went to the San Francisco courthouse to bear witness to this miraculous and fantabulous day!

There was a worship service in the park across the street, which we attended. And in the middle of the service, a bunch of young white folks showed up holding signs of protest. They did not speak. They just stood there holding their signs.

I've been to a lot of different kinds of protests and vigils over the years—against racism, against war, pro-choice, Take Back the Night, a candlelight silent march of hundreds when Matthew Shepard was killed, a vigil outside San Quentin against the death penalty—and I've been to a lot of Pride events where the right-wing zealots have shown up. I have been yelled at, verbally threatened, and egged (they missed!). I know from news reports, other activists' stories, and so on that things can turn bad quickly. In my head, I began making plans for safety if physical violence started.

We eventually figured out they were from some church. The irony of them interrupting a worship service was not lost on me, and I began to get angry at them and the hypocrisy of the situation.

The choir began to sing "I Ain't Afraid," by Holly Near. I needed to do something productive with my anger, something to ground me in love. And then I turned and faced a young blondish white woman and looked her right in the eyes and I began to sing the words to her, calmly, directly, and with conviction: "I ain't afraid of your Allah, I ain't afraid of your Yahweh, I ain't afraid of your Jesus, I'm afraid of what you do in the name of your God." The service continued on, and the protestors walked away, back to their buses, without further incident.

We celebrated a lot of love that day. We were determined to make sure folks knew that at least some religions affirmed LGBTQ+ folks and were celebrating this milestone, even as we knew that marriage equality was only one of a long list of changes needed to bring more equity and justice.

A few weeks later, Lynn and I had a conversation in the kitchen. "So, um, this wedding stuff . . ." "Yes, I never thought getting married was going to be an option in my lifetime . . ."

A few more weeks went by, and we each secretly planned to propose. In July we went to Berkeley Tuolumne Camp, where Lynn had gone regularly as a child. On a short hike alongside the Tuolumne River, with nervous laughter and a few tears, we each proposed and we each said "Yes!" We went back to camp and shared the news with family, and there was much celebration!

We set an October date. We carefully created the event, queering some of the traditional rituals. Each planning conversation led to collaborative decisions that felt honest and vulnerable. We realized that in this, too, we wanted to co-create rituals of meaning and love, together and for others. We celebrated with our families, friends, and colleagues in the lovely space (including a labyrinth) of the UU church in San Jose. It was a beautiful day!

How Could Anyone

Lynn: In December of 2008, we both went before the Ministerial Fellowship Committee, the body of folks who decide if a candidate can become eligible for ordination into UU ministry. It was exhausting and difficult, as we were supporting one another as well as being interviewed ourselves. We were both cleared for ordination, but it took us some time to recover.

The search cycle started in October at that time, so we entered the search process late but we got our big binder together to mail to congregations in search. We learned only later that the transitions director at the time did not give our names to any congregations, citing the economic downturn when we asked why not. This was quite a setback for us.

We finished our internships and had a wonderful graduation ceremony through the huge efforts of the Starr King staff. Wendy conducted a choir. Our colleagues shared moving reflections. Friends and family attended. And a few weeks later, our daughter graduated high school and headed to college. Back home, we cobbled together several part-time jobs and prepared for the next round of search. It was a tough year.

Blessed to be a Witness

Wendy: Because the search system was (and still is) set up for solo ministers, we needed to create two ministerial records and indicate in each that we would work with the other as co-minister. In the fall of 2009, we updated our records and our binder packet and jumped into the fray, interested in several congregations.

Three congregations invited us to interview. One of them let us know that one of their committee members was "against co-ministry" for unspecified reasons. One said they'd be interested in us in a few years, after we got experience. The third invited us to a pre-candidating weekend. We showed up fully as ourselves, did everything we possibly could, and worked well together throughout the process. It might have been easy for one of us to say something in an interview that the other wished had been said differently or not at all, but that didn't happen. We were queerly in sync. And . . . they chose someone else.

By this time, we had gained a lot of congregational and denominational experience both as lay folks and in and after seminary. We were active volunteers in the UU Ministers Association (UUMA) and in our district. And still we were a queer couple wanting to serve as co-ministers right out of seminary, which, to our knowledge, had not been done before.

We began to question, not our call, but our UU faith. Was it simply the timing? The economic downturn impacted both search years. Was it because we were newly "minted"? Maybe. Was it because of who we are? We do not know.

We began to look instead for positions as interim or consulting ministers. We had interviews with two very different congregations: one in the East that was very LGBTQ+-friendly, and one in the West that was in one of the most conservative counties in the state; in 2008, the county voting results were overwhelmingly against Barack Obama for president and against marriage equality.

Lynn: They were both feasible, though for very different reasons. After the interviews, both search committees offered us the job. We spoke with close friends and colleagues about the quandary. A wise person said, "Choose the one that is most like the ministry you want to be doing."

We chose the Sierra Foothills Unitarian Universalists in Auburn, California. Within the first six months, leaders in the congregation wanted to know how they could go about calling us as settled ministers. A process for doing so was created, inspired by a congregation in the Pacific northwest. And eventually, the vote to call us was a resounding yes.

Being a queer couple in the land of Tea Party leaders was a tough gig. And the folks most in need of Unitarian Universalism really needed a place to be, a place to explore their spiritual path, where all were welcome. We worked hard in the congregation. We served in our local chapter of the UUMA. We went to Sacramento for protests, rallies, and vigils. We continued to deepen our learning and act on our commitments to oppose racism and other forms of oppression, and we continued to invite the congregation into this profoundly important work.

We journeyed a long way through some hard things and created some beauty and precious memories together. The congregation was in a great place and had grown quite a bit. We loved hiking in the American River Canyon with Luna, our small, shy dog, and being close to family in California. We were blessed to be witnesses to and with many wonderful people at SFUU for seven years of shared ministry.

We Who Believe in Freedom Cannot Rest

Wendy: Leaving SFUU in 2017 was incredibly hard. We miss them, still. But the economic reality was that sharing one full-time position in a smaller church while carrying large student loan debts was tricky. So we entered the search process in hopes of a new adventure, one that would allow us to try on a new kind of ministry and also improve our financial situation.

Because we had had so little success in our first two searches for settled ministry, we were nervous. Would it be better? Would we still run into resistance to co-ministry? To people who queer the binary and ministry? We were very clear that if we did not get a new position, we could happily continue to serve SFUU and try again the next year.

The process had been updated quite a bit since 2009, so we needed to update our records and create a website instead of a binder. We made our way through all the material that congregations in search had similarly posted, clicked on the ones that intrigued us, and received invitations to interview in something like twenty of them. Some things had indeed changed.

Our candidating week at the Unitarian Universalist Society of Schenectady that spring overlapped with the UUA's denomination-wide series of teach-ins on white supremacy. We made the decision to include that in our week with them. We wanted them to know who they would be getting if they voted to call us. We worked it into worship and into several of the week's conversations and gatherings.

A member of the Schenectady Search Committee told us later that, in his professional career working for GE, he had only known hierarchical systems, and so during our interviews he kept trying to see which one of us was "really" in charge. But what he saw was that we practiced what we were describing about co-ministry. We took turns. We checked in with one another. We asked questions and listened to the answers. We valued synergy over hierarchy. We still do.

Build It with Love

Lynn: As we reflect today on our love story and the queering of co-ministry, legislatures all over the country are striving to pass anti-trans bills. Police officers are still killing Black people with impunity. The weather patterns of climate change and the behaviors of capitalism are still wreaking havoc. The COVID-19 pandemic is still with us, though many are now vaccinated and in many places caseloads and deaths are decreasing. Congregational ministry has been turned on its head. Lay folks and religious professionals are wondering what the next step for building and strengthening religious community will be, in a constantly and rapidly changing world.

Wendy: For us, queering ministry, queering the(*)logy, queering in the midst of catastrophic changes all mean that we lean even more into the work of dismantling white supremacy and hetero-patriarchal culture in ourselves, in the places we serve, and in this religious tradition.

We'll continue to ask tough questions, to center the voices of people who are often marginalized and have something to teach about making the world more fabulous and just, and to grapple with the impacts of power and oppression on how we live and how we serve the Spirit of Life. And to the best of our ability on any given day, we will love the hell out of this world, for love is the primary component in our shared liberation.

We often end our shared services with something we both say together. So, in that spirit—

Both: With humble gratitude for the journey thus far, namaste, amen, and blessed be.

Postscript: We know that we are, that we exist, that we can share a part of our story because so many other queer and non-queer kin, in and beyond Unitarian Universalism, helped to make this shared queer co-ministry possible. If we had named all the beloveds (some of whom appear in this book and/or the UU Rainbow History Project), we would have reached the word limit and not shared some of our story. We are so grateful to so many people, and we hope you can feel our deep love and profound gratitude shining humbly amidst the brilliance of the rainbows you all radiate with your fabulous lives. We hope our essay might inspire future generations to live, love, and serve queerly authentically. We pray and continue to work for a faith and a world in which LGBTQIA+ folks are cherished, affirmed, and celebrated.

The Price of Inclusion

Rev. Manish Mishra-Marzetti

Unitarian Universalism has been a life-saving experience for many LGBTQIA+ individuals, including myself. And yet that experience is not uncomplicated, particularly for a gay man of color. While I have found an inclusive and welcoming spiritual home within Unitarian Universalism, that inclusion—longed for profoundly at the level of heart and soul—has come at a cost. I have had painful encounters with racism and toxic masculinity, made all the more distressing by our espoused Unitarian Universalist social justice commitments, which *prima facie* reject such behaviors outright. The conflict between what we say and what we often do leads to a collective problem: What we reject without adequate examination, evolution, and periodic revisitation, particularly in light of changing social circumstances and needs, can continue to survive and thrive covertly.

Self-Salvation: Choosing Gayness over Cultural and Religious Expectations

I stood in the middle of the Key Bridge in Washington DC during Valentine's Day weekend of 1992, wanting to end my life. I was twenty years old, and I had done everything right, perhaps too right. I was family- and community-oriented, an observant Hindu, and an overachiever at just about everything I set my heart to, except sports. That overcompensation was meant to keep people from looking too closely, from discovering that I was gay. But I could not keep that reality away from myself, and I suffered from a hidden loneliness and isolation that seemed bottomless.

I was the eldest grandson in my paternal lineage, which is a big deal in an Indian-American family. It meant that I was, potentially, the future patriarch on that side of my family. I wanted desperately to meet my family's expectations, which went far beyond academic and career success. In line with these expectations, I would, of course, marry a woman someday, a woman that my parents would help choose and approve of.

I stood on that bridge wanting to end my life because I wanted to honor my Hindu heritage, and yet I saw no way that I could do what was expected of me. My feelings of attraction for men were undeniable and intense. I had never felt anything similar for women, no matter how much I tried. My options were, as I saw them, to 1) honor my family, culture, and religion and enter a heterosexual arranged marriage (or at best a kinder, gentler, slightly updated version of "arranged"), in which I would undoubtably have relationships on the side with men, or 2) live as a gay man, which felt like the equivalent of turning my back on my responsibilities to my family, culture, and religion. Both options involved the death of things I cared about: the first option involved me dying on the inside, the second the possibility that everyone and everything I cared about could be dead to me. It felt like it would be better to just step off the bridge and end this catch-22 misery.

In that moment, I saved myself. I was a child of both the United States and India. While I had been in turmoil trying to live fully into the Indian part of who I was, there were American ways of being, thinking, and moving in me also: individual integrity, a commitment to self-learning and growth, and understandings of personal freedom and responsibility, among others. Rather than die, physically or emotionally, I chose to be gay. At first privately, then publicly. And for me, it did mean walking away, at least in my heart, from Indian cultural expectations and Hindu community. My life became mine, yet I yearned for the central thing that I felt I had to give up in the process: a spiritual family.

Communal Salvation . . . at the Price of Aesthetic Racism

As I came out of the closet, I was fortunate enough to find, almost immediately, a community of gay men, primarily white and college-aged, who embraced me and supported me in my journey. That group of men became, and continue to be, a family to me, and though none of them had the specific cultural baggage that I had, they loved and supported me through the process of accepting myself and my reality. While I made the choice to live, these men helped me find joy among the living. And . . . it was complicated.

Our country's culture and values are predominantly defined by the white people of European descent who make up the majority, and the same is true of gay male culture within it: that culture is predominantly the creation of gay white men. And while that white gay male culture was not of my design or even intended specifically for me, gosh, was I grateful that it existed. In it, I didn't have to defend or explain what I felt inside, and some semblance of what I had to walk away from—my family of origin and my community—was recreated, with vigor, gusto, and love, as family of choice.

The cost of this was building my life in a community largely defined by white gay men, in which I routinely heard the most liberal and liberated members say things like "I don't date black men" or "I'm not attracted to Asians." This is not to say that I need or expect every gay man to be attracted to every other, but I longed for the ability to talk about how our Western television, film, and other media, particularly in the 1970s and '80s, glorified blond-haired, blue-eyed men *constantly*. If a different ideal was presented, it was a dark-haired white guy with gray or green eyes. The Western ideal of beauty or handsomeness never included anyone who looked like me, and that impacted me, even as I was myself acculturated to these societal ideals.

In the white-dominated gay community I was "exotic," an interesting and different "flavor" to try out. This meant that the gay white men I met often wanted casual or short-term, primarily physical, encounters, and these encounters were routinely rife with subconscious racism. This made me feel as if I existed only for the pleasure or benefit of those men. Finding a lasting romantic relationship was difficult. I learned, through experience, that many white men considered me a less desirable dating or long-term partner. I found that they seemed to think of themselves—sometimes implicitly, sometimes explicitly—as better than me, which was a logical outgrowth of the culture's white-centered norms of beauty. Many of the gay men I met were chasing after the Ideal—the Luke Skywalker of their dreams, or some version thereof—and I was as well, reflecting my own internalization of these culturally defined images of beauty and desire.

Even so, I longed for the ability to name and talk about the dynamics that I was experiencing, what I call *aesthetic racism*: the impact of the acculturation to, and internalization of, implicit models of beauty that glorify certain racial types and physical attributes and not others. Within the white-dominated gay community of the 1990s, meaningful conversation about internalized ideals that caused harm to nonwhite members of the community was almost impossible. "You don't want to be one of those whiny minorities who see discrimination under every rock, do you?" my younger, gaslit self was asked by the white men around me over and over again.

I had traded in cultural and religious homophobia, which had been crushing my soul, for the ubiquitous and unexamined racism of the predominantly white gay male community.

This intersection of identities—religion, race, and sexual orientation—and the need to be seen, held, and valued in my multiplicity, led to my discovery of Unitarian Universalism in my late twenties. The ongoing ache in my heart at the lack of LGBTQIA+ equality in our nation found a balm in the UU services I attended every Sunday. I treasured the ability to be in spiritual community, across generational lines, and feel welcome and included as a gay man. In my home congregation of All Souls Church Unitarian, in Washington, DC, I additionally experienced a profound commitment to racial justice which was brought alive in the deeds and lives of my siblings in faith. From a place of profound gratitude, I wanted my congregation to thrive and do well, and I wanted the same for Unitarian Universalism, more broadly. In short order, I found myself in local and national UU leadership, and soon after that I was entering seminary.

Community as a Microcosm of Humanity: My #MeTooUU Experience

As liberal and forward-thinking as we Unitarian Universalists are, I need to diligently remind myself that everything that exists in the world *writ large*—every imperfection, every attitude, every failure and shortcoming—also exists among us. Whether consciously or not, whether intentionally or not, gay men of color in American society are frequently fetishized and objectified; ancillary to the predominantly white gay male community, and often for the physical pleasure or benefit of white men. Back in the mid-2000s, these larger societal realities came crashing into my UU experience at a time when I was early in my years of professional ministry.

Before the clearer and stronger professional guidelines that are in place today existed, I attended a presentation led by a senior white gay male colleague, as part of a denominationally sponsored training program. As I listened to him, I found myself reflecting on how hard it had been for me and other ministers of color to break into the ranks of professional congregational ministry. I knew that women and openly gay and lesbian clergy had encountered similar challenges when they first began entering the profession in significant numbers. My journey in ministry, still in its early days, felt so hard already, and I wondered if this colleague, who had survived and succeeded in our vocation, might have wisdom to share. A longing for guidance and mentoring arose within me, and so I screwed up my courage, approached him, and asked if we might meet so that I could share my professional journey with him. An immediate "yes" was offered—I was thrilled—and he invited me to meet him at his hotel later that evening. (Everyone in this program was staying at the same hotel, and so I didn't overthink the suggested location.)

We met as planned, and I shared with him that I wanted to talk about my journey as a minister of color and how hard that journey continued to be. I said I hoped that he, a more senior minister who had navigated barriers and hurdles as an openly gay clergyperson, might share with me how he persevered; I hoped to learn from him and wondered if he might professionally support and guide me. He offered me cheap box wine and we began talking, but the vibe was off. I wanted to talk about professional journeys and career advancement, and he kept steering the conversation away from those topics. I began to recognize that what I had thought was ministerial charisma was actually a come-on.

I felt trapped. This was not why I had sought time with this individual, and I had no idea how to extricate myself. I felt the vulnerability of the identities that I was holding as well as the reality that

I was a newbie in professional UU ministry compared to this man's significant seniority. Everything suddenly felt precarious. I didn't want to offend someone I perceived as more powerful, someone who could possibly harm my reputation and even my career if he got angry with me. But at the same time, I absolutely did not want anything romantic or physical with him either. I proactively mentioned my fiancé (now husband), and how much I loved and adored him; he countered by telling me that he was in an open relationship and that his husband didn't care what he did on the side. He said that he needed to get out of his work clothes, and proceeded to, indeed, change into more comfortable ones. Despite the availability of a private bathroom, he got completely naked in front of me, exposing his genitalia. After changing, he then sat in a chair near me and began inching closer and closer, until he placed his hand on my inner thigh and attempted to aggressively kiss me. Nothing I'd said had indicated attraction, much less consent. Seeing no other recourse, I abruptly stood up and indicated that I needed to leave. As I extricated myself, his tone changed; he was put out; he was frustrated and angry at my not giving him what he desired. I returned to my room, utterly devastated by how thoroughly I had been objectified. I spent the rest of the night, into the next morning, on the phone with my fiancé, unable to sleep, crying and feeling like my trust, my collegiality, and my physical boundaries had all been horribly violated.

I reported this experience to the program leadership, and later through our UU professional ethics channels. It was clear to me that if such a gross breach of professional roles, trust, and physical boundaries had occurred with me, it was probably not the first time and it would probably not be the last. I felt I had a moral duty to protect others from the harm that I had suffered. I used the official channels available to me to try to do so, and what I experienced as a result only harmed me further.

As a movement, we would have readily recognized the harmful impact of a white male minister sexually harassing a female congregant. But my experience was greeted with confusion. Was this situation a "conflict" between two covenanted colleagues who needed to work things out directly with one another, or via facilitation, and re-covenant with each other? Were the more senior colleague's actions "unethical" or merely "distasteful"? What makes unwanted intimate or sexual touch automatically a violation of clergy ethics? Is it even possible for a minister to engage in physical and sexual misconduct with a colleague minister? Isn't such misconduct something that occurs between a minister and a congregant? Would unwanted sexual advances be less troublesome if the two parties were equal professional peers? Apparently this specific set of circumstances (the sexual harassment of a male UU minister by another male UU minister) had never been formally reported before, and so the language of our then existent professional ethics was endlessly discussed, dissected, and interpreted.

Meanwhile, as a brown-skinned minister whose parents were immigrants to this country, I sat with the impact of being treated in the manner in which I had been by a powerful white male colleague. I imagine—given the broader white gay male community's at times condescending attitude toward gay men of color—that I was supposed to feel thrilled, maybe even honored, that a powerful white man had taken sexual interest in me. However, I felt unseen for who I was: a member of a racial minority in a predominantly white denomination struggling to succeed in our shared profession; one who had been seeking guidance, support, and mentorship. I felt devalued and dehumanized, as if I existed for this white man's pleasure and benefit: an exotic, brown-skinned sex toy. And when he didn't get to use me for his pleasure, when his desire couldn't find fulfillment, he was mad. An ordained Unitarian Universalist minister treated me this way.

The racialized objectification and toxic masculinity that existed in the broader white gay male culture also existed in our ranks, and not just within Unitarian Universalism as a whole, but within our faith tradition's senior spiritual leadership. Disillusionment was heaped onto the pain that I already felt, and more pain was still to come.

The senior colleague hired legal counsel to represent him in the ethics investigations that occurred and conversations in professional circles buzzed that a younger, inexperienced minister must surely have overreacted and misinterpreted the more established colleague's actions. As human beings are at times wont to do, Unitarian Universalists who knew little about the situation began airing their own opinions, saying it was unfair that an immature younger minister was dragging an esteemed colleague through the mud over a misunderstanding.

How, I wonder, is a program leader getting naked in front of his junior colleague, visibly exposing his genitalia, a misunderstanding? How did my newness in the profession of ministry have any bearing on the fact that he did not care enough about me to inquire whether I was even attracted to him (I was not), or whether I wanted intimate physical touch from him? How did I misunderstand his violation of the trust that I automatically had in him, by virtue of his being in a role of leadership? I misunderstood nothing. My newness in the ministry impacted the situation in only one way: I was afraid for my career, afraid of the overt and covert ways a more senior white male colleague might retaliate for my reporting his unethical behavior. And the nature of predation is that those who aggressively cross boundaries look for and prey on those who are vulnerable, such as those holding marginalized social identities. They believe that vulnerable people will either give them what they want or shut up and stay silent, intimidated by the multiple power differentials. In this case, those power differentials included racial privilege, access to financial resources (which could fund legal representation), and his seniority in our shared profession.

I did what I could do, at the time, through official UU channels. I did not have the financial resources to lawyer up as he had, so beyond filing ethical complaints, I stayed mum, believing that as a younger brown man I stood no chance in a public relations or social media battle against a more established and powerful white man. For many years I kept my profound pain and my sense of personal violation largely private, even as this individual continued to minister in our tradition.

But we are in a different time now. With immense love and appreciation in my heart for all who have similarly claimed their voice and named their pain in service to furthering change, I now claim my personal experience as mine, to share (or not) as I feel called. This is, perhaps, one small thing that I can do to demonstrate that toxic masculinity should not silence any of us. It causes enough harm as it is; we need not let it silence us as well. Equally important, gay men should not get a "pass" on unhealthy behavior, being shown forbearance on the grounds of their minority status on one axis while they leverage privileged status on others, such as whiteness, maleness, or access to financial resources.

Moving Forward

Here in the first half of the twenty-first century, as we confront the many challenges before our nation and the wider world, good-hearted people like you and I are engaged in deep soul-searching, assessing what we have collectively and individually done well and what we have missed. As one gay Unitarian Universalist of color, I feel profound and abiding love for our tradition. My gratitude and joy for what we have collectively done to affirm, and fight for, the worth, dignity, and rights of LGBTQIA+ individuals runs deep. My experience of who we Unitarian Universalists are, in that regard, has been so life-changing, so inspiring, that it has helped propel me into the spiritual leadership of our movement.

And we have missed things that we need to account for. Toxic masculinity is not acceptable, certainly not at the hands of trusted spiritual leaders. Racism and patterns of thinking and relating that perpetuate othering, less-than-ing, and other individual or collective harm are not acceptable. These ways of looking at the world (including our societal ideas of beauty, attraction, and relationship) are directly connected to implicit cultural messaging that begins early in life. We Unitarian Universalists can model and teach better ways of honoring our collective humanity, better ways of living into healthy relationship, than our broader culture does or ever will.

We Unitarian Universalists pride ourselves on being the people who look ahead. We see ourselves as the vanguard, the people who are always *semper reformanda* ("always reforming"), helping our society to collectively learn and grow. That self-image is not undeserved; there is much historical accuracy to it. I invite us, I need us, to continue being that people—not so much for me, at this age and stage of my life, but for my Black children and other UU children like them, growing up among us, who deserve to know that they are worthy of dignity, respect, and love in ways that our larger US culture does not affirm. None of us is an object, none of us is the exotic other, none of us is expendable. We all need each other.

There is work to do, beloveds. *May the momentum of our collective work bring to life the genuine inclusivity we all need.*

Failing Forward

Lessons from California's Marriage Equality Proposition

Rev. Dr. Jonipher Kūpono Kwong

On May 15, 2008, I got a call from the local news station in Hawai'i wanting to conduct an interview in my backyard. The California Supreme Court had just ruled that not allowing same-gender couples to get married violated the state constitution. At the time, I was serving as the minister of 'Ohana Metropolitan Community Church (MCC) of Honolulu (the group had agreed to disband a couple of months before, but I don't think she knew that). MCC is an LGBTQ+-affirming Christian denomination founded by Rev. Elder Troy Perry in 1968, the year before the Stonewall Uprising. I told her how proud I was that Rev. Perry, who had been fighting for marriage equality since the 1970s, was one of the plaintiffs in that case, and that people of faith do indeed support marriage equality, which was counter to the dominant narrative at the time.

Little did I know this would be the message I would bring back to the Golden State a few months later, when I began working as an interfaith organizer for California Faith for Equality. One of the key founders of this group was the executive director of the Unitarian Universalist Legislative Ministry of California (UULM-CA), Rev. Lindi Ramsden. As a matter of fact, UULM-CA provided the 501(c)(3) umbrella for this fledgling organization.

It was imperative for a progressive religious coalition to be a part of the campaign to educate the religious communities about marriage rights, because opponents of equality—a coalition of the Church of Jesus Christ of Latter-Day Saints, the Roman Catholic Church, and several Evangelical groups—had gathered enough signatures during the summer to introduce a ballot initiative, Proposition 8, that would amend the state constitution to define marriage as between one man and one woman. It became one of the most polarizing constitutional amendments in California's history.

We knew it was going to be an uphill battle, and I was doing my organizing work in some of the most conservative parts of Southern California: Orange County and San Diego County. I was organizing in Long Beach as well, but the problem there was apathy. There were plenty of queer bars in Long Beach, and LGBTQ+ folx were fairly well assimilated into the broader community. The general feeling there was "There's no way this hateful proposition would pass in liberal California, so why not sit this one out?"

In Orange County, on the other hand, thirty-two of its thirty-four cities had voted in favor of the previous ballot initiative enshrining marriage discrimination (Proposition 22). The scant handful of religious organizations that were openly supportive of the LGBTQ+ community banded together, hosting the largest phone bank for the anti–Prop 8 campaign, which took place at Orange Coast UU Church in Costa Mesa, where over two hundred volunteers showed up to talk to voters the week before the election.

Orange County is used to having high numbers of church attendance. There were more megachurches there than anywhere else in the country—and almost all of them were extremely conservative. I remember meeting the associate pastor of one of those churches around 2009 or 2010. He understood what it meant to be an outsider, having grown up as a "gringo" missionary's child in Latin

America. He was sympathetic not only to the LGBTQ+ community, but to the Muslim community as well, arranging joint picnics for his church and the Muslim community in Orange County to encourage interfaith dialogue. We began dreaming about similar events for his church and the LGBTQ+ community to promote the common good, such as building a house together for Habitat for Humanity. Along the way, perhaps the two sides could begin to open up about their values and what makes us tick as human beings—to find common ground.

Unfortunately, this joint service project didn't take off. That minister's position was "eliminated" due to a budget shortfall that year. I'm not sure if there was more to the story than that. I sometimes wonder how much his views on openness and inclusion ran counter to those of the senior minister, who was a vocal opponent of marriage equality and whose extremely homophobic remarks were quoted in the media. Moreover, his denomination as a whole has been unabashedly antiqueer (and antiwoman, and antiblack) all along.

Relationship-building and starting a dialogue would not have happened overnight anyway. That's the problem with elections—the time crunch of needing to change people's minds by the first Tuesday of November. The pastor of another megachurch in Southern California, this one with a predominantly Asian and Pacific Islander congregation, understood this. One of his former church leaders came out as a gay man, and along with the pastor, put together a controversial forum in May of 2008 that was very well attended. His goal was to hold both perspectives together through some kind of "middle way." After all, there were different viewpoints within his own household: he voted No on Prop 8 and his wife voted in favor of it. He claimed what we needed was "convicted civility," meaning that we could maintain our deeply held beliefs and values while still being kind and respectful to those we disagree with. Doing so would let us remain at the table together, both metaphorically and, as in his home, literally.

I wonder if "convicted civility" is possible anymore, in an age of social media and extreme polarization. Goodness knows politicians haven't been able to model this notion in decades, let alone religious institutions. Pastors face the added complication of having their ministry and livelihood on the line. Congregants tend to vote with their checkbooks and/or their bodies; pastors who move "too far out" risk losing both their jobs and their congregations. That was certainly part of the reticence about supporting marriage equality.

This Asian pastor had the extra complication of traditional Asian culture. Even without the Christian overlay, Confucianism highly values the cohesion of family in a heteronormative way. A male child faces particularly strong pressure to produce an heir and carry on the family name. This was certainly the case for me. Part of what made it difficult for me to come out was my fear that I would be alienated from my family or bring them shame.

In my family's worldview, saving face is far more important than any individual's ability to choose a life that will make them happy. Perhaps second- or third-generation Asian Americans tend to have a more progressive mindset, but I am a first-generation immigrant. I remember my mom's fears that her friends would read about my work for marriage equality in the Chinese newspapers. It would be perfectly fine to make the *LA Times*, but not the *Chinese World Daily News*. I constantly struggled to balance self and community, honor and shame.

This balancing act was one of the reasons many of my Asian friends didn't want to join a UU church, even though their beliefs and values probably aligned closely with Unitarian Universalism. It is often difficult to leave the church of our upbringing because that's the community that gave us life, where we may feel we belong, even if its theology is extremely repressive. For many of us, family has to come first, even if that means sometimes sacrificing our true selves.

Over the years, however, I have come to realize that life is too short to live it without authenticity and to worry about what others think or how they'll judge you. What's more important is to live love out loud before it's too late. For me, this took the form of performing three weddings during what has come to be known as California's second "Summer of Love," when same-sex marriage was legal in the state from May until November of 2008.

One celebration during that time was for my former boss, a white man who had been with his Chinese partner for more than a decade. The marriage ceremony took place at a beautiful secluded garden in San Diego's Balboa Park, a popular location for weddings. There happened to be a band there at the same time, and when they saw us line up for the wedding, they started playing "Here Comes the Bride," creating an awkward moment when they realized there was no bride! Thankfully, they quickly recovered by playing "Chapel of Love" instead.

A few weeks after that memorable event, my former boss was diagnosed with brain cancer, and he died a few months later. I was honored to have performed that service for them in front of their friends, expressing their authentic selves and their committed relationship to the world. Marriage wasn't just a piece of paper that gave them more rights than a domestic partnership would have, but rather a societal validation of their worth and dignity as human beings. I can still picture my former boss smiling from ear to ear as he said "I do." The next milestone celebration would be the celebration of life service that his husband had to arrange for him so soon afterward.

There are marriages that are planned, and there are the unexpected ones that find us. I was sitting in the Long Beach office of the No on 8 campaign when a lesbian couple walked in with their four-year-old son. They asked my colleague for a yard sign, and as they chatted it came out that they had just come from obtaining a marriage license at the county recorder's office and were looking for an officiant. They belonged to Soka Gakkai, a lay-led Buddhist sect.

My colleague nudged me and outed me as a minister, and I awkwardly explained I was a Unitarian Universalist minister and I would need to bike home, get my script, and come back. They politely reassured me that a simple service would suffice and I just needed to be my authentic self—no fancy words required. So I gathered up everyone in the office, seven LGBTQ+ secular activists and organizers, and I did my best to channel all the weddings I have done in the past. Most of all, I spoke from the heart, wishing this family all the blessings life could offer them. By the time they were exchanging rings, there was not a dry eye amongst us. I don't think it was anything I said! Rather, it was that we were pulled away from pragmatic political strategizing and reminded of why we were doing it: affirming the public acknowledgment of love that had been denied to us for far too long and protecting that loving family as much as we could. Spirit definitely descended upon us that afternoon as we witnessed love in action.

The No on 8 campaign failed to stop the ballot measure, but it did build deeper trust between LGBTQ+ secular activists and people of faith. The LGBTQ+ community has borne centuries of spiritual abuse by organized religion, which has led to not just spiritual homelessness but sometimes literal homelessness, as well as trauma, despair, and even suicide. We knew, however, that we needed people of faith on our side. As much as religious institutions needed to set aside their homophobia and transphobia, so too did secular activists need to set aside their "faithphobia." Organized religion has much to atone for, but it can also have much to offer.

To that end, California Faith for Equality created a curriculum called the Faith Partnership Project (FPP) to foster a covenantal, instead of transactional, relationship between LGBTQ+ organizations and faith communities. Before the election, for example, LGBTQ+ organizers would sometimes stand outside houses of worship with their clipboards, asking for donations and volunteers, without ever stepping inside to attend a service. FPP asked both activists and religious people to be mindful and respectful of one another and not to vilify one another as a group; it invited everyone to practice deep listening and find common ground when possible. It became a rich opportunity to learn and grow from one another and planted a seed for long-term transformation.

Still, the No on 8 efforts failed. There was no sugar-coating the pain of an election defeat. Yes, the country elected its first African American president (who didn't support marriage equality at the time, but thankfully evolved), but I still sank into depression for a few days. I was grateful to have a boss who gave me space to grieve and to be surrounded by clergy friends who journeyed with me all along the way, an unwavering faith that reminded me where the arc of the moral universe bends, and most of all, a loving family who supported me no matter what.

It wasn't a compete defeat. There were some wins, including the huge phone bank I mentioned earlier. More than half of the phone banks for the No on 8 campaign were held at houses of worship, most of them Unitarian Universalist. We flipped two more cities in Orange County to the No on 8 side. The Asian community moved a remarkable eighteen percentage points on marriage equality over eight years since Prop 22 passed, from opposing it to supporting it.

However, anger at the loss unfortunately led to scapegoating. African American voters were blamed (even though there weren't enough black people in the state to significantly affect any election).

Protests were held outside houses of worship, including the Mormon temple in Los Angeles. The younger generation of queer activists blamed the more established LGBTQ+ political groups for running a poor campaign, spurring a few months of infighting within the LGBTQ+ community.

We held so many postmortems I stopped counting, but the one that had the greatest impact for me was the debrief at All Saints Episcopal Church in Pasadena that included all the faith stakeholders and a couple of secular LGBTQ+ organizers. We lamented the racism of claims that all black churches were antiqueer and not including the API community in key conversations as well as the exclusion of faith communities in key decision-making processes throughout the campaign. We made a commitment to "fail forward" by telling our stories boldly and having the courage to build as many relationships and coalitions as we could: not just preaching to the choir, but truly engaging with people with differing theologies. We vowed to explore the intersectionalities of oppression. We renewed our commitment not just to an election cycle, but to the unwavering belief that in the end, love wins. If love doesn't win, it's not the end yet.

The result was that national LGBTQ+ organizations established entire departments and roles dedicated to dialogue with people of faith. Many mainline Protestant denominations eventually softened their stances on LGBTQ+ issues and became more inclusive. LGBTQ+ activists began working for faith-based organizations such as No More Deaths, which works to protect and support immigrants crossing the deadly Arizona deserts. More research and focus groups were conducted to better understand the theological stances of historically Black churches. The Asian American community raised money to study how different racial communities can be approached on LGBTQ+ issues. Three queer women activists (Alicia Garza, Patrisse Cullors, and Opal Tometi) founded the Movement for Black Lives, expanding upon the 1960s civil rights movement to make it more inclusive and intersectional. (The original movement had always had a subtext of homophobia and transphobia, erasing the LGBTQ+ identity of folks like Bayard Rustin.) Spirituality and sexuality were no longer disconnected but became entwined, and where cis white privilege had often been leveraged within the LGBTQ+ community, now some LGBTQ+ groups put racial justice front and center.

Prop 8 taught us the valuable lesson not to take anything for granted. We were defeated, but it was a narrow defeat and a temporary setback. Ultimately, even a conservative Supreme Court saw that loving, committed relationships entered into in good faith are important not just to society, but to humanity's spiritual growth and evolution as well.

Meeting the Moment

Rev. Laura Smidzik

On November 7, 2012, an article on the Minnesota Public Radio website led with this announcement: "In an emotional and historic contest, Minnesota voters defeated the constitutional amendment to ban same-sex marriage." By that time, thirty other states had legally denied marriage rights to same-sex couples. This was a hard-won victory.

On the night of the vote, a large group of constituents and organizers gathered to hear the final results. Our family was included in a news segment on KSTP, a local television station. The voice-over said, "Lesbian moms Laura and Linda Smidzik say the campaign was won one conversation at a time." Then the camera focused on our son, Quintin, who was still in high school. A band across the bottom of the screen flashed "Quintin Smidzik, son." He was wearing his orange "VOTE NO" t-shirt, his voice was a bit hoarse from yelling with joy, and he was glowing! He said, "I used to tell people I had two moms and they just looked at me like I was . . . they had no idea. But now that everyone is supporting me, it is just the best feeling in the world."

I did not grow up in Minnesota. My spouse, Linda, and I moved to the Twin Cities in 1991, just a few months after we held a wedding ceremony in San Francisco. At that time Minnesota was seen as a progressive state, although it has historically fallen disgracefully behind in measures of racial equality and would later become known internationally for the murder of George Floyd. We chose the Twin Cities because they had a vibrant queer community. By the time we had kids a few years later, Rainbow Families, an organization for LGBTQ parents and their children, had been founded by a Unitarian Universalist, Deborah Talen. And even before Rainbow Families, there was the strong LGBTQ organization OutFront Minnesota, which in 1993 worked with legislators to pass a human rights bill that protected people from discrimination in housing, public accommodations, and employment based on their sexual orientation or gender identity.

State senator Michele Bachmann began trying to add a restrictive definition of marriage to the state constitution in 2003. Fortunately, many progressive faith communities were ready to engage. OutFront Minnesota saw faith communities as a critical component of their political organization. In a 2007 article for the independent news outlet *MinnPost*, Monica Meyer, OutFront's public policy director, said that "far from being a luxury, the participation of faith communities in the move toward GLBT equality is vital. In fact, it's difficult to imagine how we could push the movement forward without those voices." The Twin Cities are home to four large Unitarian Universalist congregations and several smaller ones, all within a few miles of one another. UU ministers both there and throughout the state have been intentional about forging professional and personal connections with one another. Ralph Wyman launched the Minnesota UU Social Justice Alliance (MUUSJA) in 2006 and was seasoned in faith organizing by the time the amendment was on the ballot six years later. UU congregations were active and visible throughout the years, organizing youth and adults to attend and speak at rallies for LGBTQ rights at the state capitol.

My own journey led me through a decade of leadership in the queer community, at the end of which I decided to attend seminary. I knew that I wanted my faith to be at the core of my work for justice. I was the ministerial intern at First Universalist in Minneapolis when the Unitarian Universalist Association's General Assembly (GA) was held in Minneapolis in 2010. Rev. Meg Riley, director of the UUA's Advocacy and Witness programs, received a grant from the UU Funding Program to put together a multitiered organizing effort in support of marriage equality. Working with what was then the UUA's Standing on the Side of Love program, we launched our work at GA. We arranged for GA attendees to march from the convention center to the park where Twin Cities Pride was being held that weekend. Two brides in a chariot led a river of people wearing yellow Standing on the Side of Love t-shirts through the city streets and into Loring Park, where local clergy led a spirited rally that included leaders from many faiths, testimonies of those who were impacted by marriage inequality, and musicians. It was such a poignant and joyful day!

By 2011, the Republicans had secured majorities in both houses of the legislature, and in May they passed a bill that called for a voter referendum on the amendment the following year. OutFront Minnesota immediately joined with other progressive organizations to form Minnesotans United for All Families, with the goal of defeating the ballot measure. All of the progressive faith leaders and offices also began to shore up resources; MUUSJA hired me and Lena Gardner, who is now the executive director of Black Lives of Unitarian Universalism (BLUU), as interns. I never saw anyone's ego get in the way of the work. We knew that this "marriage moment" was an opportunity to deepen Minnesotans' understanding of how an inability to legally marry threatened the security of same-sex couples. Our immediate goal was to defeat the amendment, but at the same time we realized we were building more compassionate and informed citizens.

By December 2011 MUUSJA had created a campaign name, UUs Out for Marriage Equality (UUORME), and a plan to take advantage of this historic moment. Our strategy was fourfold: we would ally with interfaith and secular organizations that shared our goals, raise public awareness of how our governments and communities denied justice to LGBTQ families, articulate a powerful moral public policy grounded in our Unitarian Universalist faith, and work toward the just treatment of LGBTQ relationships. We chose leaders and designed an action plan, with specific messages designed to target particular contexts, such as faith-based action and statewide organizing. They stressed the importance of compassion, the power of courage, the potential to bend the arc of justice, and the importance of building alliances for future work as well as the present moment. "What do we call on when we are tested?" we asked ourselves and each other.

The large multifaith worship and organizing events were particularly powerful and motivating. In September 2011, we filled Hennepin Avenue United Methodist Church with people from many faiths for a carefully planned event that would feature a PowerPoint presentation displayed on large screens high up on the walls on each side of the chancel. I remember being charged up that we had finally arrived at this big night . . . when the place went dark. Totally dark. No one could get the electricity back on, but we were determined to go forward, so candles were brought to the front of the sanctuary and the speakers projected their voices as loudly as they could. The darkness drew us all closer together and heightened the sacredness of the space.

We also had endless meetings with interfaith leaders. Many of us were trained in leading workshops on how to have a conversation about marriage. We led trainings in congregations of a variety of faiths. We did role plays, worked to reduce anxiety (it's not easy for many Minnesotans to have difficult conversations), and helped people identify their own stories about love and what they believed Minnesotans most valued.

The UUOFME team—director Ralph Wyman, Jane Bacon, D'Ann Prior, Jenny Thompson, Lena Gardner, and I—regularly met for breakfast meetings. We gathered UU ministers to contribute to the work, distributed poetry and prayers (including writing some ourselves), set up a Facebook page, and created testimonial videos. We made sure to reach out to all of the UU congregations and fellowships in the state to make sure they had what they needed to do their own organizing. We convened monthly calls from the library at First Universalist. We talked strategy, arranged trainings, set goals, and supported each other's efforts. It was amazing to hear reports from throughout the state and to feel the growing momentum. One of our strategies was to have members of UU congregations fill out cards committing themselves to a certain number of conversations about marriage equality. White Bear UU Church in Mahtomedi commemorated these commitments by creating a colorful paper chain, in which each loop represented a conversation, and hung it to crisscross the ceiling of their social hall!

At the same time, the religious right was also on full offense, launching commercials, sermons, rallies, donation drives, phone banks, and bumper stickers to get the amendment passed. Archbishop John C. Nienstedt sent an anti-equal-marriage letter to parish priests; some read it from the pulpit and others took it as a call to action. Nienstedt also distributed four hundred thousand DVDs in advance of the 2010 gubernatorial election, urging Catholics to support the amendment. Still, not all did so. Many displayed yard signs saying "Another Catholic Voting No." Lucinda Naylor, an artist who had a part-time position as artist in residence at the Basilica of St. Mary in Minneapolis, was fired for asking people to send her their copies of the DVD so that she could use them to create an art project in response to the archbishop's message; she collected more than two thousand.

I was one of the leaders mobilizing congregants at my home church, Unity Church Unitarian in Saint Paul. However, I did not assume that just because people were Unitarian Universalists they supported same-sex marriage. The May/June 2004 edition of *UU World* had run a cover article on the topic; the cover photo showed a streamer-festooned SUV driving away, with the words "FINALLY MARRIED" blazoned on the back and the license plate reading "LUV WINS." The edition that followed included a note from the senior editor, Jane Greer, saying, "Out of a total of thirteen letters, two protested the image of the SUV on the cover, four were in favor of same-sex marriage, five were opposed, and two were on matters related to same-sex marriage. This [small number of letters] is surprising for a topic that has drawn so much response in the past. The July/August 1994 issue, which ran a package of stories on homosexuality including a photo essay on commitment ceremonies, elicited a record response from readers with about half of the letters running positive and half negative—and none of them dispassionate."

I was the author of one of the "pro-marriage equality" letters submitted to the *UU World* editor. I wrote because I was asked by Rev. Janne Eller-Isaacs, my minister from Unity Church—Unitarian, who was aware of the disproportionate number of negative letters. I was surprised to learn that members of our progressive faith were ambivalent and even opposed to marriage equality. It was a humbling reality check. Fortunately, many Unitarian Universalists now talk about how their opinions about LGBTQ equality have changed over the years.

Following the defeat of the amendment in November 2012, the Democrats gained a majority in both the Minnesota House and Senate, and in May of 2013 a bill was passed making same-sex marriage legal. The law went into effect on August 1, 2013. First Universalist Church of Minneapolis held what Rev. Jen Crow, who is now senior minister there, recently referred to as "The Big Gay Wedding" on the following Sunday, August 4. Sixteen couples were married in a joint ceremony, and the congregation wrapped them in love and celebration!

Faith communities, and Unitarian Universalists in particular, were instrumental in meeting that moment in history and securing life-changing rights for same-sex couples in Minnesota. We continue to draw strength from that effort and victory as we create congregations that hold people in their full belovedness and fight for everyone in Minnesota to live full lives, protected by both state and federal law.

Loved into Being

HP Rivers

When I first visited my home church, Westside Unitarian Universalist Church in Farragut, Tennessee (a suburb of Knoxville), in 2010, the minister, Rev. Mitra, told me she believed in God on Monday, Wednesday, Friday, and alternate weekends. I didn't believe in God at all.

I was raised kind of Catholic and kind of nondenominational Christian in East Tennessee, though I never got around to my first communion and tended to be more excited for after-mass brunch with my grandparents and great-grandmother than for church itself. When I turned to the Unitarian Universalist church at seventeen years old to prove something to the boy who dumped me for not being Christian, I got much more than I bargained for.

That same minister who didn't believe in God every day also told me that we never know what someone is going through. She told me people come to the church for answers and meaning and purpose, often while enduring something soul-shakingly difficult. I've found that the kinds of answers people tend to be looking for are not so easily produced in the Unitarian Universalist tradition, where every seeker is charged with finding their own answers and truths.

There is a sacred safety in that freedom and in this beloved community.

I've found that people sometimes retain the traditions they were born into as a convenient means of belonging, but don't strive to live up to those traditions' ideals. Though I know this happens to an extent in Unitarian Universalism, I've found that most Unitarian Universalists do strive to live up to the ideals we claim, though they are lofty. We are not perfect; we have all stumbled over our own ambition at times, and we will all do so again, but for the most part, we are all trying our best.

At the time Rev. Mitra first welcomed me into the church, she was declining to officiate weddings. This was in 2010, five years before marriage equality became law nationwide, and she was abstaining from officiating wedding ceremonies in protest of legal discrimination against same-sex couples. The Westside congregation already had a long history of queer advocacy; in 2006, Westside joined several local organizations in taking out a half-page ad in the *Knoxville News Sentinel* opposing Tennessee's new discriminatory marriage law. Westside first requested Welcoming Congregation status from the UUA in 2008 and proudly maintains that status to this day. And when the rainbow flag was stolen from our church sign around 2012, Rev. Mitra led us in marching and singing "We are standing on the side of love" as we replaced and rededicated it. Westside's rainbow sign has been stolen, shot at, smashed, and defaced many more times since then and is always replaced and rededicated with love.

I am just beginning to realize what an incredible blessing it is to belong to a spiritual community that supports and affirms all people.

I am just beginning to realize what an incredible blessing it is to belong to a spiritual community that supported and affirmed my queer identity long before I even acknowledged it myself.

My parents did not express views on queer issues until I did. In seventh grade (around 2005), I had to report on a current event for my social studies class. That was when I first learned about the gay rights movement, through an article about a state that had just legalized same-sex marriage. I was moved to my core in a way I would not understand for years to come, appalled that people were being denied rights because of their sexual orientation. It seemed ridiculous to me, and I was eager to share my findings with my classmates.

I was not prepared for the hate, emboldened by out-of-context Bible verses my peers would respond with.

I was not prepared for my father to reiterate that hate when I told him about the experience later, expecting some sort of reasonable explanation and reassurance from the person whose opinion I cherished most.

In the same moments that I began to realize who I am, I was taught that who I am was not acceptable—not to society, my peers, my family, or some vague notion of God.

In the past, I have joked that since I came out later in life, I didn't get my "theater kid" phase. The older I get, the more I understand I actually spent nearly a decade putting on the best performance of my life in an attempt to make myself more safe, lovable, and worthy. I was never explicitly told that I am inherently lovable and worthy until I found Unitarian Universalism—and I never really believed it until my beloved community loved me into being, reintroducing me to the miracle that is my existence and marveling at it when I was too broken to see it for myself.

I had joined Westside at seventeen and been an active member for over a year, but then fell away for about two. I returned soon after learning I was pregnant with my son and slowly became more involved after he was born, gingerly finding my place again among the loving community I desperately wanted to be ours.

A lot had changed in three years. The kind man who sat next to me on my first visit had passed away. The minister and director of religious education had both moved on, and new people had filled the positions. The elementary schoolers I had taught in religious education were taller and more brilliant than I could have imagined, though I was completely unsurprised to discover they were blooming into engaged and empathetic young adults. There were so many new faces, and in many ways, it was a completely new place—but it still felt like home.

The day I returned to Westside—pregnant, anxious, and heartbroken—I didn't know what to expect. I had disappeared without a word into a depressive and self-destructive spiral, abandoning my teaching duties and my new community. I was worried that I would be scolded for falling away or, worse, that I wouldn't be remembered at all. But I didn't have to worry long.

Before I even reached the front steps of the church, one of my former religious education students was flying out the front door and into my arms. She threw her arms around my neck, and even though she was now a proper preteen, it was as if she was still the little girl who used to sit next to me in worship, and I knew I was home. That day was, appropriately, the congregation's annual ingathering and water communion service, and I settled into my seat still pregnant, anxious, and heartbroken, but keenly aware that I was exactly where I needed to be.

I have done more healing and growing as a part of that community than I have or ever could have anywhere else. I went back to school as a part of that community when my son was only six months old. I graduated from community college with my associate's degree in social work two years later, and my church family were the ones cheering loudest at my graduation. I got my life together and named my call to ministry as a part of that community. I went no-contact with my family of origin as a part of that community. I came out for the first time ever as a part of that community.

Actually, I came out in the minister's office on a sunny Tuesday afternoon in September 2018 during a pastoral care session.

We were talking about generational trauma, and Rev. Carol guided me in a meditation in hopes of quieting the constant chatter of insecurity in my mind.

Once the stillness was achieved, a Truth bubbled to the surface, and I laughed.

"What was that?"

"Nothing."

"No, what was that?"

"I can't—"

"Yes, you can."

I took a deep breath and smiled for incredible relief and for knowledge that I was in an absolutely safe place to speak my Truth.

"I'm super fucking gay, dude."

"Congratulations."

Not many people can say they came out as gay in a minister's office in the Bible Belt and were met with love and congratulations, but that is exactly what happened to me.

Absolutely every queer person should be able to have such a positive, uplifting coming out experience.

Absolutely everyone should have access to an affirming and loving spiritual home where they can unapologetically live their truth.

I marched in my first Pride parade with Westside just a few months later. In the moments before I came out to Rev. Carol, I had felt the trauma and shame of my ancestors leaving my body, and now I felt their profound joy and abiding love as I marched through the streets of downtown Knoxville, my beloved hometown, with my spiritual community, especially with the queer elders there.

I was euphoric as we marched, standing as tall as my inner eleven-year-old as they boldly claimed their truth before their social studies class in the only way they knew how. It was safer for me to simply claim allyship for a long time, but nothing compares to the raw and exhilarating ecstasy of owning myself and my true nature.

I know I was not the first person to sit in that office and proclaim their holy truth, nor will I be the last. That office has hosted several ministries over the years and will surely host many more. I think about my pastor's predecessor declining to officiate weddings until marriage equality became law, and I wonder about legacies. I inherited a burdensome and beautiful legacy—from my family, from society, from the Universe—and a responsibility to do everything in my power to make the world safer for those who will come after me. And I gratefully receive that duty.

No matter how many times it takes, no matter how many times the vows are broken or the path is troubled, you will always find me marching back to replace the flag that has been stolen. I will put it up again and again, offering a prayer of song to the Universe, "I am on the side of love."

For all of the grief, all of the wonderful and worrisome considerations that my identity puts upon my existence, there are still moments that take my breath away: the way that young queer people look at me in my clergy collar, with the same wide, hopeful eyes that I used to look at older queer people with; the privilege of witnessing my best friend's transition, the gift of knowing he looks more like himself today than he did the day we first met, the honor of becoming a safe person for others to share their truth with, the aching, soul-deep knowledge that I will always be a little bit afraid, but I would rather live with that fear than live in the closet again.

Even with so much complexity, how could I ever be anything but proud of how far I've come?

One of the great spiritual answers I have found for myself on my own free and responsible search for truth and meaning is that we are all a reflection of the same Divine Love. Whatever we choose to call this Source, it is a part of all of us, and it does not care how we worship or who we love. It is entirely unconditional.

This Love transcends any scripture or tradition, any walls we have built around our hearts and between ourselves and others. This

Love is the Godde I believe in, not only on Monday, Wednesday, Friday, and alternate weekends but at every moment of every day. May we all embrace this Love in a way that meets our needs, may we all allow ourselves to be embraced by it, and may we embrace one another as loved, whole, and worthy fellow travelers who are trying our best to live up to the ideals we claim—always.

Prophetic People

Rev. Jami A. Yandle

Revelation is not sealed.

The feverishness on the floor of General Assembly on June 24, 2017, peaked as I tremulously approached the microphone to propose my bylaw amendment updating the Second Source from "prophetic women and men" to "prophetic people." I had traveled over a thousand miles, taken vacation days from my job, received a scholarship from my congregation to help with funding the trip, and worked for nearly three years in pursuit of the next seventy-five seconds. With sweaty palms and waves of nausea, I took a deep breath, leaned into the trust and love I have for my people, which made me believe this change was even possible, and introduced the motion. It was seconded without hesitation.

I then spoke in favor of the new wording I had drafted: "Using language like 'women' and 'men' reinforces the gender binary, which fails to acknowledge and does not fully embrace the experiences of gender-nonbinary and transgender people nor the gender fluidity of cisgender people. I wish to thank the churches that rallied in support of this movement and got their petitions to the UUA. I wish to also acknowledge those who have come before me, particularly womanists and feminists who gave so much to be included at the table alongside men. And now it is our turn to continue that work in order to ensure a more inclusive world for our children and youth so that they know that they are loved and embraced here."

After I spoke, the time for discussion commenced. Pro and con microphones were set up for delegates to voice support for or concern about the proposal. At the pro mic, members of an organization I am proud to be part of, Trans Religious Professional Unitarian Universalists Together (TRUUsT), gathered to read an official statement and lend their support.

Then it was time for the delegates to vote.

A proposed change to the bylaws would normally have gone to a study commission for further review after its initial approval at GA. I chose the riskier route of trying to bypass the commission by calling for a direct vote; if four-fifths of the gathered delegates at GA voted to approve bypassing the study commission, the proposal would then move to the final stage of adoption. No one would be able to propose changes or debate it further, and the 2018 GA delegates would vote on its final adoption. It was a bold move but, if successful, would save years of time. As I was preparing to propose the update at GA, many people had told me that it seemed so sensible they didn't see why it hadn't been done already, which gave me confidence that the study commission was unnecessary.

When the vote was called, it took me a minute to gather the nerve to turn around and look at the gathered delegates. All I saw was a sea of yellow cards—yes votes—held high in the air, waving in celebration. The delegates voted by an overwhelming majority to bypass the study commission and adopt the new language. The assembly hall erupted in cheers and clapping. A smile broke out on my face for the first time that day, and my spirit was filled with joy.

I felt invincible that day, but the process of revision had actually begun years before.

I read our Seven Principles and Six Sources before becoming a Unitarian Universalist, encountering them first on our website and then as I sat in a pew and leafed through the hymnal. I knew that for me to fully commit to the path of Unitarian Universalism, I needed to feel included and seen, to feel that I was a visible and a vital part of this living tradition, and the Second Source's binary language of "women and men" did not include me or so many others like me.

In 2015 I wrote to the meeting planner for General Assembly, asking them to update the language of the Second Source. I remember feeling surprised that this was something I had to do, surprised that these progressive people I so much wanted to be a part of were living with this glaring and jarring wording. I could not stop wondering why someone had not already noticed and fixed it. The meeting planner got back to me swiftly, agreed the language needed an update, and explained that this wording was in the UUA bylaws; updating that was a bit more complex than just changing a few words on the UUA website and in the hymnal. They directed me to the website of the UUA bylaws, and I quickly learned that the first step toward updating a bylaw was a submission detailing the new wording. But submissions could only be proposed by the UUA Board of Trustees, the General Assembly Planning Committee, the Commission on Appraisal, or at least fifteen certified member congregations, and the submission had to be received by the UUA board 110 days prior to the opening of General Assembly.

I believed that Unitarian Universalists would support the update and that delegates would support it at GA, and since our governance is based in congregational representation, with congregations holding ultimate authority, the obvious way to begin the process was by working through congregations. I set out immediately to obtain fifteen petitions from certified congregations stating their approval of the update. I first asked my own church at the time, First Unitarian Church of Toledo, and the Board of Trustees was in full agreement that the change was overdue. Our board president at the time, Terry Acocks, was so enthusiastic about signing the petition and returning it to the UUA that I felt confident other congregations would have that same kind of energy, and I carried my church's support forward with me as I sought fourteen more petitions across the nation.

I am a hospice chaplain who works long hours, and I am on call a lot. I did not have the time or energy to create and update a website, or to organize teams of people to help spread the word. I got the word out grassroots style and by asking churches one by one when I had time, mainly through email, often in the middle of the night during my on-call hospice shifts. My approach worked; I soon learned people are more than willing to help, and all one has to do is ask. So many of my colleagues forwarded on my requests, and I remain deeply grateful for their help in making the bylaw update happen so swiftly and smoothly.

On December 6, 2016, the meeting planner informed me that fifteen petitions had been received, and the update would be placed on the business agenda at the 2017 General Assembly in New Orleans for national vote. After delegates voted to approve the language, the wording update moved into its final stage, a vote at the following year's General Assembly.

On June 22, 2018, at the Kansas City Convention Center, delegates voted much as they had in 2017, with an almost supermajority voting yes. The official language of the Second Source was updated from "prophetic women and men" to "prophetic people," so that it acknowledged "words and deeds of prophetic people which challenge us to confront powers and structures of evil with justice, compassion, and the transforming power of love."

I began this journey with the goal of full inclusion of all gender identities and expressions, as well as of children and youth. And yet I know that this language update was only part of a much larger transformation that I and so many others continue to work toward. It was and still is up to the people to support and show up for trans and nonbinary persons in our congregations, our communities, our Association, and our world. Our religious tradition had not witnessed a successful proposal to update our covenant of the Seven Principles and our Six Sources since 1995. Yet our covenant lives with us, breathes with us, and the second we allow it to collect dust we are outside the intention of its very creation. Updating the second Source invited more people into covenant with our faith and its communities and brought our sacred promises to life in the modern world. We must continue on this journey to widen the circle, to invite and include all persons into our covenants, and to build beloved community together for centuries to come. Revelation is not sealed. May this statement become a prayer and a practice, not simply a tenet of our faith.

From the Archives

Editor's note: The following sermons were written years ago and later offered as submissions for this collection. I have not made any significant changes; some authors requested some minor changes to correct errors or typos, which I did make.

Believing in Fairies

Rev. Dr. Myke Johnson

Editor's note: This sermon received the Skinner Sermon Award in 2001. Another version of it appears in Myke's book Finding Our Way Home: A Spiritual Journey into Earth Community.

A friend of mine heard a story while she was visiting Ireland. A short time before, an airport had been planning to build a new runway. On the proposed site of this runway there was an old hawthorn tree. It was gnarled and majestic, and the people in that area understood it to be an ancient fairy tree.

Unfortunately, the airport managers didn't care about this: they made plans for it to be removed. However, when they tried to hire someone to do the job, none of the local workers was willing to cut it down.

Still thinking like a corporation, the airport managers decided to bring in outside workers. The workers arrived, and one man gathered some of their equipment and started out toward the tree. When he got close to it, he tripped and fell. The other workers found him gripping his right arm in pain. It was broken. His buddies brought him into the local hospital for treatment and then went back to their own town. The airport managers decided to change the plans and move the runway.

The fairy tree was not cut down.

Believing in fairies. Could it be the tree actually was a fairy tree? Or did the beliefs of the people make it so? I remember watching the movie *Peter Pan* as a child. There comes a moment when the tiny fairy, Tinker Bell, having drunk the poison intended for Peter, begins to fade and die. She tells Peter that she can get well again if children believe in fairies. Peter appeals to all of us in the audience, "Do you believe? Clap if you believe!" Clap if you believe in fairies. Perhaps, like Tinker Bell, fairies cannot exist in our reality unless we believe in them.

This year is the sixteenth anniversary of my coming out as a lesbian. I never cease to be amazed by that transformation. When radical lesbian women came into my life my whole reality changed. It was like enough people clapping and Tinker Bell springing into view. Someone was celebrating lesbian existence and I, too, began to be able to exist as a lesbian. To claim the word *lesbian* for myself was to leap over a vast chasm, or to cut through a thick barrier. To claim the word *lesbian* was to cross a raging river into an entirely new creation.

I came out at the late age of thirty-one, after a five-year process of struggle and transformation. In the reality I knew in my younger days, gay people, like fairies, did not exist. In fact, when I was growing up, during the 1950s and 60s, I never even heard the word *lesbian*, and *gay* only meant happy.

I never saw us on TV, read about us in a book or newspaper, or learned about us in school. As a girl in a Catholic family I had two possibilities for my life path: I could become a wife and mother, or I could become a nun. I never even imagined the possibility of lesbian.

The Jewish feminist poet Adrienne Rich has written, "the whole chorus throbbing at our ears like midges, told us nothing, nothing of origins, nothing we needed to know, nothing that could re-member us. Only: that it is unnatural, the homesickness for a woman, for ourselves."

Only: that it is unnatural.

When I went to college, one of my best friends slowly revealed to those close to him that he was homosexual. This was a great torment for him, and for all of us who loved him, because according to Catholic teaching, homosexuality was against the laws of nature. Gay people were never meant to exist. And if we did exist, we were identified as unnatural, a disorder, a mistake, a problem.

So much has changed in the last thirty years since I was a teenager and young adult. One generation! Now it is hard to imagine that I didn't know about the existence of lesbians or gay men. Now we are easily found in books and newspapers, and on prime-time television. There are gay and straight alliances among high school youth. Vermont last year [2000] became the first state in the country to grant civil unions to gay couples. In Massachusetts, we are in the midst of a similar legal suit to extend the right to marry to same-sex couples. We are here together, worshipping in a community that welcomes gay people as members and as one of your ministers.

So much has changed. For me, it seems like a miracle. One, I am still amazed that I exist as a lesbian at all. And two, it is amazing that we celebrate being queer. There are still so many people who condemn us as unnatural. But in all of our various identities, as gay men, lesbians, bisexuals, as transgender or transsexual, we are creating realities where we believe in each other and ourselves, and that is changing everything.

We celebrate ourselves as queer. I choose that word consciously—a word that has been used to put us down—it is a word that has been reclaimed. I hold vivid images of young people marching and shouting: "We're here, we're queer, get used to it." In our reality, it is an identity of value. To celebrate ourselves as queer we have often had to risk every other valuable thing in our lives. Family, jobs, friends, safety. This thing that was considered a problem has become the pearl of great price. This is amazing to see. How did we go from being outcasts to celebrating and believing in ourselves? How did we go from being outcasts to demanding that reality make a place for us?

We couldn't have done it without the foundations laid before us. I am thinking about all the great liberation struggles of this last century. I am reminded of that powerful moment in the 60s when the rallying cry for African Americans became "Black is beautiful!" Claiming the power to name what is valuable. Claiming the power to believe in themselves.

Liberation theology expresses it this way: The divine is revealed in the struggle of the oppressed for liberation. The location of ultimate value has shifted. People went from being the bit players in someone else's drama to being the stars of their own. And it was like wildfire sparks lighting up so many more transformations among the ragged communities of outcast people. Claiming the power to name what is valuable. Claiming the power to believe in ourselves.

That is what happened for me, too. I found the divine in the midst of the women celebrating lesbian existence. Some of us called her "goddess." Some of us had no name to describe it. But we experienced a sacred power when we seized the courage to kiss the body of another woman.

Something shifted. It no longer mattered whether we were welcome at the table of the society that excluded us. We were in a new reality and could no longer be denied.

Adrienne Rich celebrates that moment when we call each other into existence. "This is what she was to me, and this is how I can love myself—as only a woman can love me. . . . Two women, eye to eye measuring each other's spirit, each other's limitless desire, a whole new poetry beginning here."

Was the tree in Ireland actually a fairy tree? Or did the beliefs of the people make it so? Those of us who believe in gay people are in a battle over reality. There is something going on here which is more than a simple tolerance for diversity. Those of us who believe in gay people are like sailors in a mutiny—and the ship we struggle over is reality itself.

Gay people have more in common with fairies than just the name gay men are sometimes called. Those of us who exist at the edges of reality have learned that reality is not an immutable and solid thing. Reality is capable of being turned inside out, toppled and tossed upside down. There are more realities than we know, not always only what we can already see. But reality is definitely linked to what we believe in.

African American lesbian poet Audre Lorde writes, "For those of us who live at the shoreline . . . who love in doorways coming and going in the hours between dawns . . . For all of us this instant and this triumph We were never meant to survive."

Those of us who believe in gay people are in a battle over reality. Eight years ago [1993], I received a letter from my younger sister. Her words were words that too many of us have heard from the people closest to us, from the institutions of our society. She wrote, "I pray for you night after night. . . . I do not believe people are born gay or homosexual. It is a lie from the devil, and I cast the devil out of you in the name of Jesus. You shall be made straight and whole when you accept Jesus as savior and Lord. Homosexuality is wrong! And as your sister I don't want to lose you to the devil."

Those of us who believe in gay people are in a battle over reality. We are often under assault even from those who are closest to us. How much guilt, despair, and shame have gay people carried in our guts because of their definition of reality? How many gay people have killed themselves in the pain of that reality? How many gay people have been killed, through the violence and hate of a society that refused to include us in their definition of reality? The stronger we grow, the more we also face a backlash. This year [2001] in Vermont, state legislators are trying to take back the right to civil unions. In Massachusetts we are fighting a defense of marriage act which would prohibit any legal benefits for same-sex couples. There is something about being queer that threatens everything my sister, and others like her, believe in.

Why is it so frightening? Sometimes it seems so silly to me. When I look at my life and love, and those of my lesbian and gay friends, we seem so ordinary and gentle. Nothing to be scared about. Much of the gay rights movement has been trying to convince people we are just like everyone else.

On the other hand, I don't want to so easily sacrifice the power and mystery of our difference. As much as we claim our connections, what we really have to fight for is the necessity of our difference. We are not the same as everyone else. We never will be. Most of us, like the name of a Boston band, are "adult children of heterosexuals." We will always be a minority, coming into our families like changelings, because we do not quite resemble our parents. By its very nature, queerness will always be linked to the mystery of difference. Even when we get close to settling on definitions among ourselves, things keep shifting and changing. There is always an outlaw spark which keeps reigniting. Paula Gunn Allen, a Native American lesbian of Laguna Pueblo and Sioux heritage, speaks of the "life-long liminality" that is part of being queer. The word *liminal* describes those things that are at the threshold, the place where we cross over into another place. She says, "Transformationality is what constitutes the sacred moment, the process of changing from one condition to another." Queer people are sacred inasmuch as we are involved in the shifting of reality.

There is power and mystery in our difference. We have been hearing a lot about DNA in the news recently, and the project to map the pattern of human DNA: DNA is the genetic code that determines the characteristics of our bodies and the hereditary traits that will be passed on to the next generation. A few years ago, I watched a science documentary on Boston-based GBH Channel 2 called *Origins*. It told the story of the original discovery of DNA. Two scientists named Watson and Crick were able to figure out the basic chemical model of its structure. DNA consists of a double helix made up of recurring pairs of four substances: cytosine and guanine, and adenine and thymine. CG and AT for short. There are several billion of these in our human DNA strands. All of life, every species of plant and animal, from viruses and bacteria to the largest whales in the sea, is formed from these same inner codes, like a four-letter alphabet, really, spelling out billions of different words. There is only a one-percent difference between the patterns for humans and the patterns for chimpanzees. Even yeast DNA is similar enough to interact with our own in certain ways. CG and AT, GC and TA.

Within this interconnected web, there is a lesson about difference. According to the evolutionary theories, all of the diversity of life grew from small mutations in the code . . . a C instead of a G, perhaps, one in a million times. The narrator described them as like small spelling errors. That's what caught my attention. Did he say all of the diversity of creation sprang from small spelling mistakes?

It reminded me of the patterns in rugs made by the Navajo, or Diné, people. It is traditional for the Diné weaver to purposefully leave a small flaw in each rug. The Diné understand this as a way of expressing respect, that what is made by humans can't be perfect. Only the Great Spirit can make perfect things. But the meaning I was wondering about was different. If creation itself is born of the small flaws, then perhaps it is the Creator herself who causes so-called "mistakes" to come into being. The mistakes are the seeds of the next new thing. The mistakes themselves are sacred and holy. There is a parable here for the deviance of queer existence. Rather than trying to get everyone to see how ordinary we are, rather than trying to make sure we fit in, what might happen if we believed in the power of our deviance?

And this is a question not just for gay or transgender people. This is a question for anyone who doesn't quite match the norm. Anyone with disabilities. Anyone who isn't white. Anyone who is deaf or hard of hearing. Anyone who is "too fat" or "too thin." Anyone who is on the edges, out of a job, homeless. Any of us who are not exactly perfect. Any of us who feel caught between realities, who don't really fit the way we are supposed to.

What changes when we stop seeing the so-called mistakes as problems? What changes when we are open to the sacredness of aberration? What happens when we believe in ourselves and in each other?

According to Chicana lesbian writer Gloria Anzaldua, primal cultures saw a magic aspect in abnormality and so-called deformity. Maimed, mad, and sexually different people were believed to possess supernatural powers.

In the Jewish and Christian scriptures, we read, "The stone which the builders rejected has become the keystone" [Psalm 118:22 and Mark 12:10].

When we believe in each other, all of reality begins to shift. When we believe in each other, in all of the mystery of our deviance, we align ourselves with the ancient power of creation. The power that brings forth new forms out from the material of the old. The power that experiments, evolves, mutates, transforms. When we believe in each other, we reveal a vision of the divine as an ever-changing, ever-creating force. When we believe in each other, we are like a spelling mistake on the way to creating a new reality. When we believe in each other.

A Different Church

Rev. Gail R. Geisenhainer

Editor's note: This is an excerpt from a sermon delivered at General Assembly in June 2006. It was included in the 2010 edition of the Unitarian Universalist Pocket Guide.

I was forthrightly evangelized into Unitarian Universalism. I was thirty-eight years old, living in Maine, driving a snowplow for a living and feeling very sorry for myself when a friend invited me to his church. He said it was different. I rudely refused. I cursed his church. "All blank-ing churches are the same," I informed him, "they say they're open—but they don't want queer folk. To heck with church!" My friend persisted. He *knew* his church was different. He told me his church cared about people, embraced diverse families, and worked to make a better world. He assured me I could come and not have to hide any aspects of myself. So I went.

And I dressed sooooo . . . *carefully* for my first Sunday visit. I spiked my short hair straight up into the air. I dug out my heaviest, oldest work boots, the ones with the chain saw cut that exposed the steel toe. I got my torn blue jeans and my leather jacket. There would be not a shred of ambiguity this Sunday morning. They would embrace me in my full Amazon glory, or they could fry ice. I carefully arranged my outfit so it would highlight the rock-hard chip I carried on my shoulder, I bundled up every shred of pain and hurt and betrayal I had harbored from every other religious experience in my life, and I lumbered into that tiny meetinghouse on the coast of Maine.

Blue jeans and boots. Leather jacket, spiked hair, and belligerent attitude. I accepted my friend's invitation and I went to his church. I expected the gray-haired ladies in the foyer to step back in fear. That would have been familiar. Instead, they stepped forward, offered me a bulletin and a newsletter, and invited me to stay for coffee. It was so . . . odd! They never even flinched!

They called me "dear." "Stay for coffee, dear."

I stayed for coffee. I stayed for Unitarian Universalism. Over time, the good folks of that church loved up the scattered parts of me and guided me from shattered to whole, from outcast to beloved among many. And those folks listened to me. I and my life partner became their poster children for the brand new Welcoming Congregation program, designed to help congregations live into their values for effective welcoming of LGBTQ people. And they went on to provide important local pastoral and legislative ministries to gay folks in Down East Maine. We walked together and we helped each other grow.

Please don't think the transition was smooth or swift. These were not imaginary superheroes, they were human beings. And this was the mid-1980s. During the worship service on my second or third Sunday, a woman stood during Joys and Concerns to announce that all homosexuals had AIDS; all homosexuals were deviants who could not be trusted with children, public health, or civil society. All homosexuals should be quarantined, packed off to work camps to provide useful labor for society and keep their filthy lifestyle and deadly diseases to themselves.

As the member spoke I slowly sat upright from my customary slouch. I tucked in my arms, looked furtively around to see who might be glaring in my direction, and tried to remember if I had parked my truck facing in or out in the parking lot. In its journey of covenant, this congregation had just stumbled onto an important crossroad. But as Joys and Concerns continued, not one person made reference to the call to quarantine all homosexuals. The pulpit that morning was ably filled by a student from the local seminary. At the end of the sharing, the seminarian made a brief comment to assure us that not all the sentiments voiced that morning represented the whole congregation, and that was that!

Now I was at my own crossroad. I left quickly after the service. But what about next Sunday? Would I go back? Why on earth would I go back? That would be . . . well, you fill in the word—dangerous, stupid, foolhardy, looking for trouble, probably hurtful. But back I went. I was in the throes of learning my first lessons of being in covenant with a congregation. When we covenant to walk together through all that life brings, it means that, when things get ugly, we don't walk away. Oh, how we may want to walk away! But our covenants call us to abide and work things through.

The next week, the regular minister was back. The service began as usual. I tensed up when Joys and Concerns came around. Someone announced something like a birthday, I can't fully remember. But I vividly remember that, one by one, folks stood up and awkwardly announced that not everything said last week was right, or true, or representative of who we were as a Unitarian Universalist congregation.

The crossroad had been engaged. The direction the congregation would take was being chosen. This congregation would not get stuck in conflict, mired in name-calling, or diverted from its gentle, steady trek toward building the Beloved Community. Our aspirations were unfolding, one voice at a time.

The congregation had passed a test. One among them had used language that depersonalized and endangered others. She tried to create a class of less-than-human persons toward whom violence would be acceptable. The congregation gently refused to follow. But an even more extraordinary and wonderful thing happened. The congregation also refused to depersonalize or dehumanize the original speaker. They did not start calling her names: "That homophobe!" "That gay-basher!" None of that happened. While the speaker tried to turn homosexuals into objects to be manipulated, the congregation never referred to her in a way that was less than embracing and respectful of her full humanity.

Later, in that same church, I opened the hymnal to find words attributed to the Buddha: "Never does hatred cease by hating in return." He taught, "Let us overcome violence by gentleness. Only through love can hatred come to an end. Never does hatred cease by hating in return."

My friend was right. His church was different. He forgot to tell me that, at his church, I could be in for a wild ride some Sundays. But he was still right. His church really cared about making things right for everybody.

A Deep and Continuous Call

Rev. Dr. Gwendolyn Howard

Prelude

In 1859, not long before his death, Theodore Parker wrote an extended letter to his congregation that was then published as a brief memoir entitled *Experience as a Minister*. While reading Parker's work during my first year of seminary at Meadville Lombard Theological School, I came across these words: "In my early boyhood I *felt* I was to be a minister, and looked forward with eager longings for the work to which I still think my nature itself an 'effectual call,' certainly a deep one, and a continuous." I understood exactly the feeling Parker was writing about, for I felt the same from childhood.

When I was born in 1954, words like *transgender* and *intersex* were unheard of. It would not be until nearly a decade after graduating from seminary that I would identify as a transgender woman—first to my spouse, then more publicly. (And it would be even later before I discovered what I had suspected: that I could also be described as intersex due to some underlying conditions.) Yet even as a child, I knew I was not the "boy" everyone assumed I should be. With this awareness growing up, I knew that the Roman Catholic faith of my upbringing was not going to be a place where my call could ever find expression.

After college and a short career in public broadcasting, I decided to enter programs at Meadville Lombard and the University of

Chicago in the autumn of 1982. Upon graduation with a master's degree and a doctorate in ministry, I was first hired by Cambridge Forum (a project housed at First Parish in Cambridge); then I was called to the Universalist Unitarian Church of Peoria, Illinois. I left after two years to become the settled minister at St. Paul's Universalist Church in Little Falls, New York, where I served for five years. During my time in Little Falls, I could no longer hide from my own identity. I came out to my spouse, Pat, and together we struggled with what this would mean for me, her, and us. After some time, I began discussions with a UUA district official on what I ought to do professionally.

Little Falls would be the last church I would serve full-time.

I left at the beginning of 1996. Twenty-four years later, the congregation voted to name me minister emerita. It was an incredible and humbling honor. On the occasion of its being formally conferred, I returned to the church for a special Sunday service. The following sermon I preached at that service describes, among other things, what happened upon my departure from my congregation.

Sermon: "Where the Journey Takes You" (September 29, 2019)

It's funny how memory works (or maybe it's just that I've gotten to the age where it doesn't work quite as well as it used to). But I can remember the last Sunday morning I preached here almost as if it were just last week. Pat had already been living in Providence, Rhode Island, for three months. I had driven our cats to their new home on Christmas Day (and let me tell you that spending Christmas alone in a car with three upset and anxious cats for almost five hours is not nearly as much fun as I thought it would be). But for my last Sunday here, Pat was back. We spent quite a little time closing up the house.

I hadn't slept much on the Saturday night before the service. And by Sunday morning I was starting to fall apart. You see, I've always disliked goodbyes and I really hate change (and yes, I do see the irony in my saying that). I knew that there would be so much about this place that I would miss (especially people). And like most ministers, I hoped that I'd really made a deeper difference (I mean, besides things like getting the carpeting and pew cushions done, or the ramp on the front of the building). And like most people when confronted with the end of a relationship, I had regrets. But I'll say more about that in a little bit.

When I got to Providence, I needed to find work. For a while I tried to find something that might fit my skills and experience as a minister. When the person in charge of ministerial settlement was in town to preach, I attended the service to get to talk to him for a few minutes. I'd known him back in the days when I'd been an intern in the Pacific Northwest. Like in many churches, when the service was over, most people lined up to say a word or two with the preacher, or maybe just shake their hand. When it was my turn, the preacher recognized me and in a bellowing voice shouted, "Welcome, brother!" (Other people in line looked at me and then him and seemed really confused.) Things only went downhill after that. Another time, I interviewed with the board of a small church that was looking for an interim. At the end of the interview, they told me how they thought I'd be very good, but they were worried about what other people in town might think. One denomination official I spoke with was very direct: He said that he wanted to be supportive of me "as a person" but also wanted me to know that I should never expect help from the UUA and that I needed to find a new career. I had a ministerial colleague tell me that she was just being "helpful" in letting me know that while she, as a lesbian, understood the struggle I was having trying to find a position as a minister, she wanted me to be "realistic," because all marginalized groups have had to "wait their turn."

I could relate more stories like this—far too many stories—but it should give you some idea of how things went. Because I needed the money, I eventually did temp work. I was employed at everything from being a TTY operator for the deaf and hearing-impaired, to being an administrative assistant in the facilities management department at a university (I actually got to learn a bit about things like heating, air conditioning, and plumbing in that job, which has proven to be a valuable life skill).

While these jobs were sometimes interesting, and while they did help pay the bills, it felt like something was missing. After all, I had always thought about ministry as not just a job, and even though it didn't seem like parish work was in my immediate future, I still felt a calling.

After lots of soul-searching, I decided that I might be able to make a difference in other ways. I was accepted into the Masters of Social Work program at Boston University. The program at BU turned out to be the right place for me at the time. I expected to go there to learn about mental health and therapy (and I did learn about those things), but the school didn't lose track of the "social" aspect of social work. I learned about communities and organizing, race, and social justice. I eventually graduated with a clinical degree, but my specialization was in group work. That was a bit surprising, I suppose, for someone like me who is really an introvert at heart. But perhaps not—after all, it does fit with my theology that the "sacred" is not something distant that is "out there" but is right here among us.

As a social worker, I did one internship with a program for LGBTQ youth (many of whom were perilously close to having to live on the streets because of being rejected by their own families). I really came to love those young people. (You know, my first taste of youth work came here.) The following year, I interned at a clinic for clients with chronic mental health issues.

After graduation I got a full-time job at a similar clinic, mostly working with groups. I quickly found that there were some clients none of the other staff liked. These clinicians would complain about these folks at staff meetings and try to avoid them unless they absolutely needed to interact. I soon found that the most troubled and troubling clients were my favorites. Yes, they could be a real challenge, but they were the ones who needed help the most. If you kept the metaphorical door open and the welcome mat out, sometimes, just sometimes, they would respond.

With my parents getting older and my dad developing heart trouble, in December 1999 it became clear that they couldn't live on their own in Iowa anymore. They were both blind and my mom had her own set of mental health issues, so we brought them to Providence. It meant that my career moved into the background as they needed so much attention and care. During the last ten years, as my mom had to enter the nursing home, I did a little bit of private practice therapy, and I was able to get some teaching jobs in higher education. I taught comparative religion, philosophy, psychology, and quite a few classes in ethics. It still amazes me when I think about how many young people I tried to help learn how to be better human beings.

It was also during these last ten years that a local UU minister invited me to become a community minister at the church he served. I was still angry with Unitarian Universalism, but when it is at its best, it is still the right place for me. I became a community minister (unpaid, of course). Later on, from out of nowhere, I got a call from a little church in Rockland, Massachusetts, and they wanted to know if I'd be interested in interviewing with their board—they were looking for someone to come and preach at their church twice a month. And to show you how much times have changed, they hired me. I began serving them in September 2014.

With reluctance, I had to quit doing that just last year. My own vision is gradually getting worse, and I could no longer drive the hour-and-a-quarter each way on Sunday mornings. But I really liked those folks. I've never truly felt at home at big, multi-staff churches with lots of programs, but I do have a special affection for small churches. (I wonder where I got that from?) They can be quirky, but they can also be powerful.

This seems like a fair amount of personal timeline for one sermon. But I did want to share with you what I've been up to since I was here. That has certainly been on my mind lately. At sunset tonight, Rosh Hashana begins. It's the Jewish New Year. Among other things, it has often been described as a time for personal reflection. And in getting ready to come here today, I've been doing an awful lot of that.

In ancient times, the turn of the new year was thought to be the anniversary of the very first day of creation. There was also a common belief in those days that we humans have a bigger hand in creation than we realize. If we did good (or, as they might have said, "followed God's laws"), everything would be fine. But if we didn't—if we didn't do what was right—we could actually contribute to the unraveling of creation itself. (Given what I see when I watch the news, I'm starting to wonder if they may be right.)

That doing wrong can be so powerful and dangerous to the very fabric of existence certainly puts all our actions in perspective. So setting aside the time of the new year and the days that follow to look back at how we've been living our lives seems like a very natural and important thing to do (and not that you need any more pressure, but it was also thought by many that God was also looking over how each of us had lived during the past year). I admit that I've been thinking about more than just the past year, but I haven't been here for a while, so I hope you understand.

By tradition, after these days of a new year and reflection (called the Days of Awe) comes Yom Kippur—the Day of Atonement. It is when we're supposed to recognize and acknowledge the wrong we've done, seek sincere forgiveness, and make amends. And that has also been weighing on me lately.

During my last year here [1995-1996], I was in the process of coming out—becoming more honest about myself and who I am. I sought advice from the executive of the St. Lawrence District. She told me she wanted to be supportive, but that I needed to leave and was never to tell this congregation about it. I was told I had to lie.

So I did.

I rationalized it by telling myself that it would probably not go well anyway, and that if I ever wanted to do church work again, I would need to do what I was told by this denominational official. Also, I was afraid.

But I was wrong. Lying to you was wrong. There certainly might have been consequences, difficult consequences, but I owed this congregation the truth. It is my sincere hope that you can forgive me for that wrong.[1]

There is something of a different nature that I also need to tell you. It is to thank you. Serving with you, I was made a better minister—a better person—than I would otherwise have been. When I got here, I found a congregation that the denomination just didn't know what to do with. It's frustrating, but you quietly persisted. Eventually I'd find myself in the position of being a minister that

---

1 Coming out and transitioning can be a very difficult thing to do: legally, physically, and emotionally. It can also ruin relationships that you might have thought were strong and healthy. For as many successful stories of transitioning that I know of, I am aware of many more that turned out painfully. What I was writing about in this part of my sermon was my relationship with my congregation. No one else can or should tell you how best to come out and/or transition. You are better at judging your own needs and safety.

the denomination didn't know what to do with. Your example was often on my mind. This church has had others (including ministers) tell you what you must do to be a typical UU church—even what your name ought to be—and yet you have quietly gone on being your unique self. It is no coincidence that I came out during my time here.

While I was here, you made sure I learned about Universalism. It's a religious tradition that was not only about individual freedom, not only about seeking the truth wherever it may lead you, but from its beginnings was a faith in the belief that whatever God is, and whatever Love is, they are one and the same, and that we need to see the holiness—the sacred—in everyone, even the least among us. You taught me about community—that church is a place of welcome, of acceptance; although it might sometimes fall short, it is, at its best, family. You may not always be in perfect harmony with other family members, but you know they will be there for you (even when you've gone far from home). Of all the places I have ever been and of all the places I may ever be, I think of here as *my* home church.

When I was working with clients who were the most challenging and the most troubled, you were there with me.

When I, along with a handful of others, succeeded in getting Rhode Island to become one of the first states in the country to recognize the civil rights of people regardless of gender identity or expression—even though everyone told us it couldn't happen—you were there with me.

When I was helping hundreds of young people learn that just being out for yourself isn't enough, and that we have a fundamental obligation to be good to one another, you were there with me.

Real, caring community. The best of what a family should be. A place where we're encouraged to believe in the redeeming power of love. A place with the quiet courage to be itself, no matter what others—ministers, or denominations, or anybody—say it ought to be. I think that is the value, the meaning, and the purpose of "church."

My life has gone in many directions, most of them unexpected. In my time here, I hope that I listened as much as I spoke. I hope I made some small contribution to this congregation. It is here that I came to do the work of figuring out just who I am. It is here that I learned what it means to do ministry (whether inside a church building or beyond its walls).

For all you have taught me and for being who you are, I thank you. Amen.

Postlude

I was drawn to Unitarian Universalism so many decades ago because of the ideals and promise which it held. My own story, unfortunately, is one in which it all too often failed to fulfill that promise and stubbornly refused to live up to those ideals. Because of this failure and refusal, the majority of my own experience as a minister never found expression in a parish. Yet I firmly believe that the best of what I have done in my life is, nonetheless, in answer to that high calling. And I know from my own experience that there are among us those caring individuals and congregations which actually do put their faith into practice, and who will lead us forward into a more free, welcoming, and loving world, if we will but follow their example.

Called to Task Divine

Rev. Thomas Disrud

Editor's note: Rev. Disrud preached this sermon on June 7, 2020, at the First Unitarian Church of Portland, Oregon, on the twenty-fifth anniversary of his call there as associate minister. It was also just two weeks after the murder of George Floyd in Minneapolis.

Eight minutes and forty-six seconds. Hearing that in the abstract doesn't sound like a whole lot of time. But then imagining that amount of time with a police officer's knee on your neck, that's a whole different story. In that context it feels like an eternity. In fact, I have to confess to you this morning that I haven't been able to watch the whole video of George Floyd being pinned to the ground for that long, crying out for help, calling out the names of those he loves. It is just too excruciating.

Yes, even watching that video for a few seconds seems to last a lifetime. Seeing the other officers standing there for all that time and not doing anything. There has been something about that video that has seemed to cut through a whole bunch of stuff. It is impossible to not recognize George Floyd's humanity and the need that rises up and to say no. This is just not acceptable. And that's how it should be. That shouldn't be anything close to acceptable or normal.

The optimist in me wants to believe that this time, with protests in so many places and involving so many people, that this time there might be a sea change. I want to believe that this time will be different, that life at some point will not just go back to normal until the next black person is killed. I want to believe that this time might be different. Maybe it is some combination of the brutality of this death and of so many deaths. Maybe it is the disruption of COVID that has made a space for the reality of this to show through for more of us than it has up until this time, including the stark reality of how much more COVID has impacted Brown and Black and Indigenous people.

But I also have to note that I, like many of us who identify as white, can essentially make a choice about that. We can choose how far we get out of our bubbles of comfort and when to retreat back in. That is where our privilege comes in. For people of color it isn't like that, I'm told. For people of color you can't turn that awareness off; you can't turn that fear off. It is something that you very much live with most or all of the time. It is a reality of life.

I want to hope that all of this is pointing toward something. I want to believe that there is some larger reckoning happening here. That we are in the midst of some kind of sea change. And as I say that, I know just how hard actual change can be. Changes in laws and policies. Changes in a culture that too often says yes to such brutality. Are those images of police officers choosing to kneel with protesters a sign? Are those statements from military leaders that the military should not be called out and deployed against their fellow citizens a sign that enough is enough?

I want to believe that maybe there is something that is different this time. And I know that even as individuals change, changing systems is even harder. That is going to take something much more sustained, something that is not going to happen easily, something that is going to take all of us being willing to say no. I want to believe that that is possible.

This was a sermon planned pre-COVID, pre-protests, to mark twenty-five years of ministry here for me. What an honor it has been to serve and to be here with all of you through these many years. This congregation has a history of shaping new ministers who come here, and I have certainly been one of those. No, it hasn't always been easy, but that's not the nature of ministry. But overall what I'm feeling is gratitude to have been able to serve this community. I consider myself extremely blessed.

And given the state of our world right now, it actually is a source of hope for me as I try to hold, as I try to make sense of, all that is happening. Ministers and congregations at their best learn and grow and make justice in the world together. They call out what's possible in each other. They make a space for all of us to ask: How is it that we choose to live in a world so full of beauty and so full of brokenness? How is it that we make sense of our individual selves, and how is it we are in relation to some greater whole? Just what does it mean for us to know ourselves to be part of a Beloved Community and to have a role in making that possible?

The first time that I heard of the First Unitarian Church of Portland was back in the fall of 1992. I was starting my second year of seminary in Berkeley and there was a lot of buzz about this congregation. It was the happening church in our denomination.

The church had just called Marilyn Sewell to be its new senior minister. The fact that a prominent church had called a woman was actually a big deal back then, believe it or not. Just a handful of other larger congregations had done that. And it also happened that at the very same time Ballot Measure 9 was going before voters here. It was an effort led by Christian conservatives to disenfranchise lesbian and gay citizens here in Oregon. It was a terrible, divisive initiative.

A friend of mine, Amanda Aikman, had come here to be summer minister that year, and when she came back to school she said something that surprised me: that I should keep an eye on the Portland church, that she thought that Marilyn Sewell and I might be a good team. Now at the time I thought—I was pretty sure—that I wasn't going into parish ministry, that my call was to be a chaplain. And having been involved only in small churches my whole life, a growing, large church seemed like it was, to tell the truth, a little out of my league. But long story short, that's what happened. And here we are now, twenty-five years later.

And when I look back at that time now, that too proved to be a time of sea change on many levels. It was a time when this congregation and its sense of self would blossom and never be quite the same. It was another time that felt as if the world might just be shifting in some fundamental way towards justice. But it wasn't easy. It was a time when queer folks were under attack, when it seemed to be permissible not only to discriminate but also to brutalize and kill. And communities of faith, many of them, were either supporting the measure or not saying anything at all about it. Too many people of faith were silent.

But for this community it proved to be a catalyst for change, both within and in its witness in the larger community. Some of you have heard the story of the wrapping of this church block with a red ribbon and the declaration of a hate-free zone. That act was a kind of spark that brought all kinds of people into this community. People wanted to be part of a faith community that said no to hate.

It was a couple years after all of that that I, a not-too-long-out-of-the-closet gay man, was called. I didn't know what it would be like. I didn't know what it would be like to come to Portland. Looking for an apartment, I met a landlord who owned, of all places, an apartment complex called the Stonewall, who said to me, when he learned that I was a minister, that he felt like he could rent to me after hearing what I did for a living. After all, he confided in me, "We have to keep out the homosexuals."

Truth be told, calling an out gay minister didn't seem to be that big a deal for the congregation. I think I was probably more anxious about my sexual orientation than most of the folks in the church. I think that's what can happen when you try to disenfranchise one group or another—they get to the point of saying, "No, we aren't going to take that anymore," and I think that's what had happened with that ballot measure. A lot of queer folks just said no. And a lot of allies said, "We are with you."

Now it would be easy to want to romanticize all this. One of the things I have learned in these years is that change does take time, and in particular real systemic change. And part of that change is realizing that we all need to change and maybe sometimes even give things up. It means being open to shifting cultures and noticing who has a seat at the proverbial table and who does not. And it means that we aren't always kind to each other.

A few months into my ministry here, I had a board member, an older straight white male, tell me that I wasn't welcome here. He even said that with my arrival all the straight men in the congregation had left, which was quite a statement. Clearly my so-called gaydar was not as accurate as I thought it was. What I eventually learned in that situation, which is so often the case in ministry, was that it really wasn't about me. I represented for him some new reality that he wasn't quite ready to accept. That's one of the difficult things about ministry, that projection piece. People tend to see the best or the worst in you, and it is too easy to get put on a pedestal. And that can be a precarious place to be. But ministers can come to represent some combination of god and parent and first-grade teacher all rolled into one. No, that is one part of ministry that I'd be glad to give up.

But I have also learned that for that real change to happen, we all play a role. And it means being willing to look at our own stuff and to not put it onto others. It means recognizing the privilege some of us have. It means making a space for those who have been on the margins to be welcomed into the center. It means seeing ourselves as part of the change we want to see.

And I believe that we can make a difference. When Marilyn Sewell had a press conference to announce that ribbon around the block and the declaration of a hate-free zone, it happened to be on the same day that the Women's Alliance met—and yes, back then it was the Women's Alliance, the group that began as the Ladies Sewing Society, the group that founded the church. They were meeting that day, and they stood behind the minister as she held the press conference. Some of them, the story goes, still wore white gloves to the monthly luncheon, and so the visual was, as the commercial might say, priceless. Here were the matriarchs of the congregation, if you will, witnessing for justice.

And the timing also needed to be right. The church in the years leading up to that pivotal time had been pretty inward-looking. The former minister had lost one wife to cancer and then, after happily remarrying, six years later lost another wife to cancer. It seemed as if the minister and the congregation went through a kind of wilderness. But there is also something in that wilderness, that searching, that was a kind of catalyst for change and a possibility of rebirth. That, too, is part of the story.

We talk about ministers having callings, but I have come to learn that institutions, just like people, have callings. They have a mission and live out that mission in the world. And sometimes we find ourselves in certain moments in history that are set apart. The church I was called to was in one of those times. I think the church we are in right now may be in one of those times. And what we do—or don't do—does make a difference. The Black Lives Matter banner on the side of the church makes that statement and bears witness today.

But part of that call asks us all to look at issues of power and privilege and change, and those usually aren't easy. It means sometimes those of us who have the power have to trust enough to give some of it up. It means adapting to change and growth. When all of that change happened here in the nineties, it wasn't necessarily welcomed by all. There was a great sense of loss for many. In fact, for some it felt as if they were losing their church. People talked about the sense of the church being one big family, and all of a sudden all these new people show up for the party, and that wasn't necessarily a good thing. And the years that followed brought the need to figure out things like governance and space needs and staffing. No, those years were not necessarily easy.

Churches, I have learned, are very human institutions, and we don't always bring our best selves to the effort. Let me be clear that my experience has very much been that more often than not we do bring our best selves, but not always. We want our church to be there for us when we experience change in our lives, and we don't necessarily welcome it when that very change is happening at church.

But there is also possibility. There is a kind of grace as, more and more, we might be able to see our own lives in the lives of others. In this case it was a lot of straight-identified folks seeing that the lives of queer folks mattered and that our destinies were somehow connected. This was a time before I had heard much about intersectionality, but it is really about understanding that oppression, in its many forms, harms all of us. It is about seeing that our individual lives, and all of the parts of our identity we bring, are welcomed and valued.

The story of this congregation has been about bearing witness to the times it is in. We talk about the founders of this church, including its ministers, but we know that they, too, were anything but perfect. They were from New England and saw the world ordered in a certain way, and they, of course, were at the top of the hierarchy. Equality for them maintained that order and it left a lot of folks out.

Rev. Bill [Sinkford] and I have, on occasion, wondered what Thomas Lamb Eliot, the first minister [of First Unitarian Portland], or Earl Morse Wilbur, the first associate, would have to say about the church being led by an African American man and an out gay man. Could they even have imagined? I'd like to think they would be proud, but truthfully the image that more often comes to mind is them turning over in their graves.

The thing about change is that, once it is happening, you don't know what doors will be opened and stay open. The wrapping of the block all those years ago was part of some larger change that would, eventually, lead to marriage equality. I could not have imagined that when I came here. I did not believe at the time that I would see that in my lifetime.

There have been many moments of grace. Back in 2004, on a rainy Portland March morning, I got a call from some of our members who had been in line since the night before at the county building. Word had come down that Multnomah County was going to issue marriage licenses to same-sex couples the next day. I will never forget the joy in that line that day. Later that morning the first couples came here to the church, and some of the women on the staff happily took on the roles of honorary mothers of the brides. I pulled together a wedding ceremony. In that first week I had the privilege of officiating at eighteen weddings. That is something I will never forget.

One of the saddest moments in all these years was seeing those marriages nullified and the backlash that happened here and all over the country that year when gay marriage was used by the Republicans as a wedge issue. It would take more than ten years before those couples could legally marry with the blessing of the US Supreme Court.

What I think I have learned in these years of ministry is that churches are very human institutions. They are a body of people who come together for mutual support and care but also to help that arc of the universe bend towards justice.

In the story for all ages this morning, Cassandra [Scheffman] talked about the origins of the flower communion ritual that came out of the Unitarian Church of Prague almost one hundred years ago. I noted that that church also had hard wooden chairs—for those of you out there missing being here in the sanctuary, do you remember them? But the minister, Norbert Čapek, also needed a way to bring his people together and for them to see the beauty in each other, and to remind them that even if they did not all share the same beliefs, there was a power in their coming together and in the recognition that they were more together than their individual selves. In these times this is one of the ways that we are staying together. And in what might be some sign of the future, we are drawing people from all of the country and even a few places around the world. What a blessing that has been in these times.

Our times are different in many ways from when Čapek offered that first Flower Communion, but that basic statement of theology is still very much alive for us today. The spirit asks us to recognize our interdependence and to recognize how our lives are connected with the lives of others. It seems so simple, and we know just how hard it can be. To get past our individual egos, to get past our fears, to get past, or at least to be mindful of, our privileges. To get past so many walls that we as individuals and the systems out of which we come. It takes a willingness to be uncomfortable. It takes courage to bear witness. It takes a willingness to trust.

The truth is that faith communities are living bodies and we are constantly working to make that circle we call the Beloved Community wider. And truth is that that can be hard work. Unitarian

Universalism's promise—and our challenge—is that honoring of the individual without it all becoming all about any one person. It is about seeing in our own lives the lives of others.

Our spiritual theme this month is Sanctuary. My hope and prayer for this institution is that it might serve as a sanctuary for all of us, a place to take shelter from the storm. But sanctuary is also a place where we go for strength, for courage. It is a place where we might find our grounding, a place where we might also begin on our path to freedom, joining with others as we go. And it means staying true to that call. It means making a commitment for the long haul.

Ultimately, we are all in this together. That means seeing in our lives the lives of the George Floyds and the Breonna Taylors. It means seeing in our lives the lives of our transgender siblings when they are assaulted for just being who they are. It means recognizing how the immigrants who are in detention, sometimes without their children, could be us. It is all about bearing witness to those we know and those we don't know. It is about bearing witness to our own hurts and fears and so many things that would keep us apart. It means committing ourselves for the longer haul because it is in that longer haul that change, real change, happens.

Is all that possible? I want to believe it is. Let us join together in that dance, that march, that all of us—all of us—might know that community we call beloved.

Let's Get Together

A Brief History of UU LGBTQIA+ Groups

Rev. Jane Dwinell

From the Spring 1975 UU Gay and Lesbian Caucus (UUGLC) newsletter:

> "When an Alabama UU Fellowship received a letter announcing a proposed mid-winter conference of UU Gays, the chairperson returned the letter explaining: 'Our fellowship does not have sexual perverts. We already lost some members because this militant minority got approval by the General Assembly. If this poster goes up we lose more members. Gay Unitarians are destroying the existence of UU itself.'"

How far we have come!

When UUGLC was formed in the mid-1970s, its purpose was to create a place for gay and lesbian UUs to find each other and work together on issues of concern. The first two projects were to lobby the UUA board to create an Office of Gay Affairs (later renamed Office of Gay Concerns) and to promote non-discrimination in hiring practices at the UUA, in congregations, and in local and state governments. The early newsletters were full of actions being taken at General Assembly, by individual congregational groups, and by secular national organizations, as well as information about more than sixty gay and lesbian Unitarian Universalists who were willing to be contacted for support. Sometimes they gave a full name and address, sometimes just a first name and a phone number.

The UUGLC was successful in lobbying for an Office of Gay Affairs, but it was not smooth sailing. For the first few years, it was unclear whether or not the Office would survive as an official part of the UUA, or whether the staff person would be paid or volunteer, part-time or full-time. There was much overlap between UUGLC and the Office—and that lingered for all the years of UUGLC (which later became Interweave Continental)—enough so that periodically there would be a newsletter article describing the differences.

But it wasn't all politics. UUGLC organized social events at General Assembly where people could just get together and know they were not alone. "Coming out" to one's family, one's workplace, and one's congregation was hard work, and people looked for support where they could find it. For many people, coming out was not an option, and a social event at GA was a gift. UUGLC also had a booth in the exhibit hall and a worship service, and held several workshops. In 1975, two hundred people attended a "Gays in Your Church" workshop, where brave panelists talked about what life was like for them in their congregational home. Homophobia was rampant, worse in some parts of the country than in others.

Chapters began to be formed in congregations and in districts. The newsletter always contained news from these offshoot organizations describing political activities, educational forums, worship services, and social events. The newsletter began listing contact information for the chapters, and the number of chapters reached a peak of seventy-five in 1991.

Time passed. The Office of Gay Affairs was secure. General Assembly began to pass more and more resolutions pertaining to the lives of gay and lesbian people. The first specific resolution addressing bisexual, gay, and lesbian people, "Discrimination Against Homosexuals and Bisexuals," was passed in 1970, and subsequent ones passed every few years, on topics ranging from continuing the Office, to services of union, protesting discrimination in the military and in employment, marriage equality, and the Boy Scouts. Members of UUGLC/Interweave often wrote, sponsored, and spoke to these resolutions.

Then in the fall of 1982, a new crisis was mentioned for the first time in the newsletter. Throughout the eighties, the newsletter was full of information about AIDS, sermons about AIDS, personal essays about living with AIDS, and eventually, obituaries of those UU activists who had died from the disease.

The most prominent of these was Rev. Mark DeWolfe. He wrote in the December 1986 newsletter:

> Learning to accept the fact that I am a person with AIDS is proving to be a slow process; it's sinking in slowly but surely. It means accepting, or perhaps just realizing, that my time here to live is limited. Limited, but still indefinite; I don't know really how much time I have, and even if I did, I would be working to make it both as long and as rich as I can. I will, of course, be doing everything I can to prolong my life; I'm not ready to give up on it yet. I'm still in love with living, with people, with the earth, too much to love to let go of life easily.

Mark died in 1988 at the age of thirty-five. The newsletter marked his passing, and the Mark DeWolfe Award was born in 1996, given each year at General Assembly to a Unitarian Universalist who had gone above and beyond to enhance the lives of queer people.

By the mid-eighties, things seem to ramp up for UUGLC. Bylaws were created, along with a more structured leadership design. An annual "Convocation" to be held in February was proposed. The word *bisexual* began to appear in the newsletter, and lobbying to add the word to the name of the organization began.

"Convo" began in 1985 in Houston. Among the business discussed was a new name. Should UU Gay and Lesbian Caucus become UU Gay and Lesbian Concerns? Or perhaps Gays and Lesbians Affirmed (GALA)? Maybe Interweave: the UU Gay and Lesbian Community? In the end, there was no name change.

These winter gatherings allowed more time for socializing, workshops, keynote speeches, and networking. Convo was held all over the US and Canada—wherever a willing member or two were up for organizing the event. Attendees generally numbered in the low hundreds, more or less depending on the size of the city. The business meeting was moved from General Assembly to Convo. It was a time to focus specifically on the organization, what was being done, and what could be done. A new logo—the familiar pink triangle chalice pin—was created.

The Welcoming Congregation program was proposed in December 1988 and then approved at Convo in 1989 as an educational tool to help congregations understand more about the lives of queer people, reduce homophobia, and create a safe space in congregational life.

Little by little, things changed for the better for gay and lesbian Unitarian Universalists.

However, adding the word *bisexual* to the name became controversial. While the newsletter didn't go into great detail about this controversy, it was palpable. Out of frustration, the UU Bisexual Network (UU Bi Net) was formed in 1991, and at the 1992 Convo, a motion to add *bisexual* to the name was tabled. Several bisexual people continued to write for the newsletter, keeping their profile and their lives in the forefront. Finally, at the 1993 Convo, there was a vote to change the name to either UU Lesbian, Gay and Bisexual Concerns or Interweave, and merge with UU Bi Net.

Interweave: Unitarian Universalists for Lesbian, Gay, Bisexual and Transgender Concerns was born. UUGLC took its place in history.

Energy increased. The board held a Long Range Planning retreat in 1993 and decided that "racism is Interweave's most pressing problem." That, too, became controversial, with pro and con arguments in the newsletter. Interweave was dominated by older, middle-class, white gay men—as it had been from the beginning—and the rough edges of change began to be seen as the organization drew more women, more bisexual people, a few transgender people, youth and young adults, and straight allies into leadership roles. Interweave struggled with racial equity, like many other UU organizations, and still does.

Marriage equality arose as the new cause for queer people. First Hawaii, and then Vermont, brought this issue into their courts and then their legislatures. Civil unions became law in Vermont in 2000, and then seven couples (three of whom were Unitarian Universalist) sued Massachusetts in 2001 for the right to marry. That right was granted in 2004. It was a heady time for LGBTQ activists.

In the meantime, the terrorist attacks of September 11, 2001, happened. Attendance at the February 2002 Convo in Las Vegas was sparse. Even though that Convo was billed as a visioning meeting and the people in attendance were very engaged, it began to feel like the beginning of the end. Subsequent Convos were also sparsely attended, and in 2004, the board began to discuss whether or not Convo should continue. By 2009, it became clear—Convo was no longer relevant. The world was different for queer people; there were many other spaces where we could gather and we no longer needed the sanctuary of a UU-only space. In addition, the 2008 recession made attending Convo a financial impossibility for many people. In 2010, Interweave members began to meet at Creating Change, the annual conference put on by the National Gay and Lesbian Task Force, and the Interweave annual meeting moved back to General Assembly.

Another death knell for Interweave was the loss of affiliate organization status within the UUA in 2007. Affiliate organization status meant that a group was given two General Assembly workshop slots, it was listed in the UUA Directory and on the website, and advertise in *UU World* at a discounted rate. Affiliate status gave an organization legitimacy. Interweave was not the only organization to lose affiliate status—many organizations did, as the UUA looked to its own priorities.

Interweave soldiered on despite these two setbacks. In 2006, it received a grant from the UU Funding Program to create a curriculum about bisexuality by myself, Dana Dwinell-Yardley, Scott McNeill, Ann Schranz, and Amy Zucker Morgenstern, which was published in 2006, and then to create a curriculum about transgender identity by Johnny Blazes and Julia Terry, which came out in 2010. The UUFP also funded Interweave from 2012 to 2015 to hire a newsletter editor and create a bigger, more professional, and theme-based newsletter, which was emailed to all members and all congregations.

But as Susan Gore, Interweave president from 1997 to 2001, said, "Organizations, like people, have life cycles." As with many volunteer-run organizations, there was a consistent cry over forty years for more people to step up into leadership positions, to put out the newsletter, to lead workshops at General Assembly, and to coordinate Convocation. Despite many board retreats, goal-setting and visioning sessions, it was simply too hard for Interweave to do everything it wanted to without paid staff. Always, there was a call in the newsletter for more donations, more members, more grant-writing possibilities. There was so much UUGLC and Interweave wanted to do. There was much work to be done. But the money never came.

The world for bisexuals, gay men, lesbians, and transgender and queer people looked one way in the 1970s and looked completely different in the 2010s. In the larger world, non-discrimination laws, marriage equality, acceptance of LGBTQ people in the military, and the repeal of sodomy laws made life better for everyone. The strength of the Welcoming Congregation program, the various General Assembly resolutions, the onset of the Beyond Categorical Thinking program (to deal with discrimination in the search for a minister), and the employment non-discrimination clause in the UUA bylaws made life safer and more welcoming for queer Unitarian Universalists. Homophobia, biphobia, and transphobia still cause harm in the world, but I don't think there is a Unitarian Universalist anywhere who would label us as "sexual perverts" "destroying the existence of Unitarian Universalism itself."

Building TRUUsT

Rev. Mr. Barb Greve,
with Alex Kapitan

If you had told me twenty years ago that within a few short decades there would be more than a hundred trans religious professionals in Unitarian Universalism, I would have been skeptical. Back then, my highest hope was that maybe—just maybe—I might live to witness a couple dozen of us serve our faith professionally. I never could have known at the time that TRUUsT, an organization of trans UU religious professionals that was still more of an idea than a reality, would so quickly grow beyond my wildest dreams.

TRUUsT was born not in a moment but over the course of several years, many conversations, and a great deal of need. As one of few openly trans leaders within Unitarian Universalism, I had personally experienced that need and witnessed it in too many others for years. Being the child of a father who worked in human resources and a mother who worked as a UU religious educator on both local and continental levels gave me a predilection for systems thinking and an awareness of denominational dynamics. After many UU leadership roles in my childhood and youth, I was hired into the Office of Lesbian, Bisexual, and Gay Concerns (OLBGC) at the Unitarian Universalist Association. The year was 1995, I was twenty-four, the Welcoming Congregation Program was five years old, and less than 8 percent of UU congregations had voted to be recognized as Welcoming Congregations, with only a dozen or so more working on the program. The call to become more LGBTQ-welcoming was not being taken up by the majority of UU congregations, due to a widespread belief that they were already welcoming enough—as long as no one felt the need to "flaunt" their sexuality.

I was out about my sexual orientation when I was hired by Rev. Meg Riley, then-director of both OLBGC and the Washington Office for Advocacy, but it wasn't until a few months after being hired that I came out as third gender/trans to my UUA colleagues. As a queer and trans person, it was frustrating to watch the mainstream UU movement slowly embrace the message of becoming more tolerant of heteronormative gays and lesbians while continuing to perpetuate oppression and exclusion toward LGBTQ people who weren't interested or able to assimilate into mainstream culture. By the late 1990s, Matthew Shepard's murder in 1998 and the burgeoning same-sex marriage movement had motivated a lot of straight, cisgender UUs to become active allies, but there was a huge amount of resistance to bisexual, queer, and trans welcome. And at state and national levels, I watched as UU public advocacy work on trans rights was intentionally sacrificed in favor of same-sex marriage advocacy work with anti-trans interfaith and lesbian/gay organizational partners.

It was an isolating time to be trans, both in Unitarian Universalism and in the wider world. Online forms of connection were in their infancy, email wasn't yet widespread, and long-distance phone calls were expensive, so trans communities existed only in hyper-local or word-of-mouth ways. And because of the way systemic oppression operates to turn people with marginalized identities against each other, there was unfortunately also a lot of infighting among the few groups that existed, which often broke down along fault lines of gender identity, race, class, ability, desire or lack of desire for medical transition, and desire or ability to be "out" or "stealth." Within

Unitarian Universalism, trans leaders were desperately few and far between. Although the denomination had made a commitment, with a 1980 business resolution, to remove barriers to employment for lesbian, gay, and bisexual religious leaders, the same commitment had not been made to trans leaders almost two decades later.

So although quite a few trans people went through seminary, were ordained, and/or pursued employment in UU congregations during the 1980s and 90s, no openly trans person was called to serve a UU congregation until 2002. I would later learn of ministers who came out as trans while serving UU congregations and were forced to leave, such as Rev. Dr. Gwendolyn Howard, and others who graduated from seminary but were rejected by the Ministerial Fellowship Committee (MFC), such as the late Rev. Erinn Melby, who was only cleared for fellowship after ten years of effort. We'll never know just how many trans leaders Unitarian Universalism lost due to transphobia—whether because they couldn't make it through the system at all, made it through only to be blocked or pushed out later, or were forced to choose between their call to ministry and living openly as their true selves.

Meanwhile, for most lay trans UUs at the time, just having a minister who didn't tell them they were going to hell was powerful. The vast majority of cisgender UU ministers were not prepared to offer pastoral care of any kind to trans people, and the most accepting of them were quick to call one of the very few openly trans leaders in Unitarian Universalism, including me, whenever someone came out as trans in their congregation. In short, trans people were referred to other trans people for support. By the time I entered seminary in 2002 at Starr King School for the Ministry (SKSM), while continuing to work (now part-time) for the UUA, Sean Parker Dennison had been counseled to call me, and I had been counseled to call Sean, at least a dozen times each—despite the fact that we had been close friends for years, ever since attending an FTM International Conference together in 1997.

It wasn't long into our friendship that Sean and I started talking about the need for an organization of trans UU leaders. We were doing our best to support each other and work for harm reduction within UU institutions, but we were too often dismissed or tokenistically relied upon as individuals. As a UUA staff person, I had fought for and provided multiple trans 101 trainings of the MFC before I got to SKSM, yet it was clear that there was a pattern of systemic oppression within the highest levels of the denomination, as well as people with personal prejudice and the institutional power to cause immense harm to aspiring trans leaders. Conversely, Sean asked for trans trainings at SKSM, and these requests were met enthusiastically by then-president Rev. Dr. Rebecca Parker.

One of the final straws for me was when, at a 2003 Western Regional Subcommittee on Candidacy retreat in California, a leader said in reference to me, "Things like that shouldn't be in our ministry." I rightly asked to be assigned to a different subcommittee, because I refused to have my ministry judged by someone who couldn't see my humanity, but my request was denied by the UUA's director of ministerial education. I suggested being assigned to the Massachusetts subcommittee instead, because that was where my permanent residence was, but was told that I was too well known there for them to judge me fairly. It was clear to me that I was being experienced as a problem or a troublemaker rather than as evidence of oppression baked into the system.

Not long afterward, Sean and I were talking, as we often did, about our frustration with the lack of proactive action to support trans leaders in Unitarian Universalism. The most visible openly trans leaders at the time were the two of us and Rev. Laurie Auffant, who had been ordained in 1999. We knew that an organization, even if it was initially just a shell corporation for a couple of us, would have more power than we did individually, because organizations were listened to more than individuals. So we decided right then and there to start TRUUsT. (We laughed uproariously when we received our first letter addressed to TRUUsT, from the UUA's office of ministerial education, asking for recommendations for trainers for yet another trans 101 training for the MFC and its subcommittees.) In June 2005, TRUUsT hosted its first lunchtime gathering at UUMA Ministry Days, a tradition that continued for fifteen years.

When we talked about what to name this nascent organization, Sean kept bringing us back to the value of solidarity and trust. There was so much animosity and distrust created by systems of oppression both within and outside Unitarian Universalism. Trans people—and other folks with marginalized identities—were expected to compete against each other for "success" according to oppressive standards. After much discussion, we decided on "TRUUsT" as a slightly forced acronym standing for Transgender Religious professional UUs Together. (To this day I have folders labeled TRpUUsT; "the *p* is silent and the *s* is small.")

One of the key challenges we had from the very beginning was who TRUUsT would be designed to serve. We felt it was beyond our capacity to serve all trans folks, and we expected both Interweave Continental and the UUA to live into their commitments to support lay trans UUs, so we decided to focus initially on trans religious professionals. We were committed to TRUUsT being not just for ordained clergy but for anyone who was serving in a professional religious leadership capacity, with particular inclusion of religious educators. Sean's dream was that TRUUsT would eventually become a multi-layered organization serving UU religious professionals, lay trans UUs, and cisgender allies.

Our goal for TRUUsT was to advocate for trans religious professionals within the institutional bodies of Unitarian Universalism and also be a place where our colleagues could gather for mutual support. For the first couple of years, we focused on providing trainings and workshops at the institutional level, including for the MFC, UUA staff, gatherings of the Liberal Religious Educators Association (LREDA) and Unitarian Universalist Ministers Association (UUMA), and staff and students at SKSM and Meadville Lombard. We also regularly tabled at LREDA and UUMA events; we had to say "come talk to us if you're interested in TRUUsT *or interested in supporting TRUUsT*," because there were so many UU leaders who didn't feel able to be publicly trans. We were surprised by the number of more seasoned clergy who came to us and told us that if they were coming out today they would come out as trans, but that they had made things work well enough to get by and wanted to simply support us from afar.

There were also a number of trans seminarians who were scared to be publicly out as trans because of discrimination. Limited as our power was, Sean and I felt that we had enough of it in the wider system to push for harm reduction and accountability within the denomination in a way that would help those coming up behind us. But there was a cost to being the groundbreakers. Being labeled a troublemaker impacted my ability to navigate through the ministerial credentialing process myself, which had long-lasting impacts on my professional development and career. Being involved in TRUUsT and trans advocacy put Sean's parish ministry at risk whenever transphobic people occupied congregational leadership roles. It was spiritually draining to have to weigh which battles to fight in terms of our energy, time, need for employment, and ethics. These ongoing tensions also strained our friendship.

After a few years of TRUUsT existing in an informal way, building relationships, and continuing to do trainings and other harm reduction, we received a generous grant from the UU Funding Program in

2007, which gave us the push we needed to bring together a steering committee. We decided to create an initial steering committee that was an intentional mix of publicly trans UU religious professionals and cisgender UU religious professionals who were trusted allies and willing to leverage their power to support trans leaders.

This new leadership body came together for the first time at a retreat in April 2008 at the Essex Retreat Center in Massachusetts. Jamison Green served as facilitator and created a powerful container for us to build community, relax and restore our souls, and also shift the paradigm to center trans experience. Much of the gathering, for me, focused on breaking the dynamic of competitive "firsts" that is so common in mainstream culture—who was the first trans religious professional, the first openly trans ordained minister, the first openly trans minister called to a UU congregation, etc.—and instead creating an environment of all being in this together. The cisgender members of the steering committee also learned what they could do to support trans UU leaders.

We held a second steering committee retreat two years later in April 2010, at St. Dorothy's Rest retreat center in California, facilitated by Heidi Green. What stands out most for me from that retreat was an exercise in which we were invited to write TRUUsT's obituary. Sean and I, in particular, were feeling so mired down in the everyday barriers faced by us and every other trans UU leader that we couldn't think of anything beyond actually being able to get ordained (me) and perhaps having a memorial scholarship for trans people in our name (Sean). Luckily the other steering committee members had more hope for the future, which is how TRUUsT's initial vision statement came to be: "Born out of commitment to the gifts, safety, liberation, and leadership of transgender people, TRUUsT is at the center of a new spiritual awakening that transforms Unitarian Universalism through worship, pastoral care, theology, education, and community to the end that transgender ministers and their ministries are thriving, and a new culture of solidarity and common purpose among Unitarian Universalists committed to countering intersecting oppressions is flourishing."

Having a more formalized leadership structure gave us the gift of no longer feeling so alone in the work, and I'll forever be grateful to those who served on the steering committee during this period in addition to me, Sean, and Laurie: Rev. Paul Langston-Daley, Rev. Dr. Rebecca Parker, Rev. Dr. Rosemary Bray-McNatt, Rev. Kim Crawford-Harvie, Rev. Gail Geisenhainer, Rev. Josh Pawelek, Rev. Michelle LaGrave, Rev. Sunshine Jeremiah Wolfe, and Rev. Anya Johnston. At every LREDA Fall Conference and every UUMA Ministry Days, we continued to host tables and be as publicly known in leadership circles as we could, but we still weren't connecting with more than one additional openly trans leader per year. We continued to do education and trainings at the institutional level, as well as instituting gender-neutral bathrooms at General Assembly in 2013. We also formed an informal advisory board populated by known allies who were waiting at the ready to use their institutional power to advocate in specific ways. Despite all of our efforts, the work still felt like such an uphill battle. Due to my fear of what would happen if I said no, I too often said yes to requests to speak, consult, lead workshops, and serve on leadership teams despite the impact on my personal relationships and finances.

From the very beginning, our dream had been to hold a retreat for trans UU religious professionals; in 2016, we were finally able to achieve that dream. The planning took years, starting at the 2010 gathering of the steering committee, but what kept us going was knowing that there was finally a critical mass of trans UU leaders and how deeply we needed to gather, share our stories, and support one another.

It felt unbelievable to me that, when it came time to invite people to the retreat, we sent invites to almost thirty people. I'd never thought I'd live to see that many trans people committed to leadership within our faith. In the end, fifteen of us were able to attend, and even that felt massive. For so long, it had been four of us—me, Sean, Laurie, and Paul—and then for so much longer, there had only been a loose network of very few others.

And so, in April 2016, fifteen trans UU leaders gathered in Pacific Grove, California, for three days, along with Kate Bornstein as our retreat leader. Two UUA staff members, Dr. Janice Marie Johnson and Rev. Sarah Lammert, also attended portions of the retreat to create new relationships and facilitate new accountability. And on the gathering's first full day, Rev. Dr. Rosemary Bray-McNatt and Rev. Dr. Sofía Betancourt visited and led us in worship, bringing blessings from Diverse & Revolutionary UU Multicultural Ministries (DRUUMM) and tales of the very first Finding Our Way Home retreat for UU religious professionals of color.

It was a transformative experience for probably all who attended. Each of us brought wounds and scars, and each of us found healing in community. We honored our rightful place in Unitarian Universalism, told our stories, and imagined our future. We created a "history wall," where we documented and wove together multiple threads of our individual stories, UU institutional history, and the wider world with respect to trans and LGBQ+ people. Collectively looking at that woven history and broader context helped heal some of the broken relationships that had been created by the wider systems and made it possible to celebrate successes. We officially transitioned TRUUsT's steering committee to a trans-only leadership body. And we brought three concrete asks to Janice and Sarah as representatives of the UUA: the creation, with TRUUsT's help, of a network or structure at the UUA to support trans people in Unitarian Universalism; holding staff who reported to them responsible for doing no harm to those in our community; and funding for a second retreat the following year.

Those three and a half days represented a turning point for TRUUsT as an organization. They created a deepened relationship between TRUUsT and the leadership of the UUA, for one thing. But perhaps most importantly, TRUUsT was now firmly a membership organization after years as a loose collection of relationships. This meant new conversations about who would be invited to join, and after much discussion and discernment, the steering committee made the decision to expand membership to all trans UUs living out a call to ministry within Unitarian Universalism. Where before TRUUsT had been inclusive only of ordained ministers, religious educators, and ministerial candidates, now it would be open to ordained and lay ministers, credentialed and non-credentialed religious educators, directors of music and church administrators, seminarians and chaplains, and more. This move was informed both by the expansive definition of "religious professional" similarly used by the Finding Our Way Home community and by the recognition that the barriers to credentialed leadership for trans people within Unitarian Universalism meant that many trans UU leaders follow nontraditional paths.

A public call to join TRUUsT articulated this expansive definition, as well as the expansive definition of "trans" that had been true for TRUUsT since the beginning. "We are trans," TRUUsT's website now read, continuing: "we are transgender, genderqueer, gender fluid, nonbinary, two spirit, intersex, agender, bigender, third gender, neutrois, transsexual, and/or otherwise marginalized in terms of gender identity." To many Unitarian Universalists, this articulation was a surprise, due to the widespread mainstream mythology that being "trans" meant being a trans woman or a trans man, period. But neither I nor Sean ever identified as anything other than what today would be called nonbinary. When we founded TRUUsT, Sean identified as genderfull and I identified as third gender. (I now identify as genderqueer.) The fact that so many UUs have thought of both of us as trans men speaks only to the tenacity of the gender binary and the continuing invisibility and erasure of people who aren't women or men. Despite our own visibility and relative power in the system compared with many others, we have never been fully understood, fully valued, fully able to push for more than the system is willing to give.

The final turning point represented by the 2016 retreat was more personal: I felt able to leave the steering committee and receive the gift of being simply a member of TRUUsT myself, secure in the knowledge that more leaders would carry the organization forward.

Over the next five years, TRUUsT's membership grew by leaps and bounds. In April 2017, twenty-seven out of thirty-nine members gathered in Palm Harbor, Florida, and by January 2019, there were sixty-one members, twenty-seven of whom attended the third membership retreat in Oracle, Arizona. This period also saw huge successes. In the spring of 2017, two trans ministers were settled in new pulpits—both called by unanimous congregational votes—and then, incredibly, seven trans ministers were called or hired into new congregations in 2019. Meanwhile, two trans leaders—myself and the late Elandria Williams—were asked to serve as co-moderators of the UUA, our association's highest volunteer leadership role.

Yet through it all, pushback, backlash, and barriers seemed as rampant as ever—whether about pronouns, bathrooms, health insurance, or any number of other basic needs for trans people. In 2018, TRUUsT partnered with the UUA to conduct a survey of trans Unitarian Universalists, and the results were deeply telling. Almost three-quarters of respondents did not feel their congregations were completely inclusive of them as trans people, and 42 percent reported regularly experiencing trans-related marginalization in UU spaces.

The numbers were far worse for the subgroups of nonbinary UUs, trans UU young adults, trans UUs of color, and the most financially insecure trans UUs.

The last five years have brought a lot of rapid change in the wider world and within Unitarian Universalism. It has been extremely heartening to see increased institutional support for trans people and new commitments to trans justice, such as the 2021 Action of Immediate Witness calling on Unitarian Universalists to respond to the escalating targeting of the trans community for political attacks and the 2024 Business Resolution that deepened and expanded this commitment. Where once I was the only openly trans person working at the UUA's national office, there are now many—and in recognition of the pressures of being trans in leadership, the UUA recently decided to contract a dedicated chaplain for trans staff. At the fourth TRUUsT membership retreat in San Diego in 2023, I arrived and realized there were more attendees I did not know than ones I knew, which was delightfully mind-boggling to me.

It's clear that we've come further as a movement than I ever imagined, and yet we are far from arriving. It is particularly troubling to me that the UUA has long considered the calling or hiring of leaders with marginalized identities as a metric of success, rather than the length and health of those ministries—and it shows. That 2019 TRUUsT report shared that the majority of trans ordained ministers who had served UU congregations had experienced being pushed out of employment. Trans women and transfeminine folk have been especially underrepresented in leadership positions. I can't help wondering what barriers and lack of supports all of the newly settled/hired trans religious professionals will experience, and my heart hurts daily for all of the trans people who find Unitarian Universalism only to experience walls where there should be doors, backs turned where there should be open arms, debates about grammar and violent stereotyping where there should be celebration of the gifts trans people bring to our faith.

If I'm honest, most days I feel weighed down by the mountain still before us, particularly in the face of today's virulent anti-trans movement. But when I think about how much things have changed in twenty years, I draw strength from the conversations I have with young folks who are celebrating gender fluidity instead of feeling isolated and without words for who they are, and in the parents whose first concern is how to advocate for their newly out trans six-year-olds rather than freaking out that their teens are questioning their gender. These moments help me hold onto hope that Unitarian Universalism will rise to meet the needs for trans advocacy and refuge in this new era. As much as I fear for what they will experience and mourn the barriers they still face, I am so blessedly amazed and grateful for those who are coming after and beside me, and humbled to think that I helped create a space and an organization that is there for them/us. It makes all of the hard work that it took to get here that much more meaningful.

Postscript

We're Not Done Yet

When I first began working on this book project over six years ago, one of my primary goals was to tell as complete a history (up to the present moment in our denomination) as possible: the successes, the failures, the complexities. While the project shifted away from any attempt at completeness, I believe the stories shared here have accomplished the goal of presenting a balanced view, with representation of successes, failures, and, above all else, complexities.

The stories in this collection celebrate the ways in which Unitarian Universalists (as individuals, congregations, and a denomination) have chosen the side of love with regard to LGBTQIA+ people and our rights. They also name where we have fallen painfully short, causing real harm to real human beings.

Here we are in 2026, and I feel compelled to name that there are still things to celebrate and things to regret. At the October 2019 conference of the UU Retired Ministers and Partners Association, contributor Jane Dwinell (who had been doing Beyond Categorical Thinking workshops with congregations for twenty-two years at that point) shared that "what people worry about has changed—people are now freaked out about [not race but] trans and queer ministers."

While many congregations have participated in the Welcoming Congregation program, it is also important to name that not all congregations have engaged equally well with the work of welcome.

Some never earned the Welcoming Congregation designation. Some did that, but have not kept up with new understandings of welcome, including the importance of being specifically welcoming to transgender, nonbinary, and genderfluid people who come into our congregations looking for a religious home where they can be fully themselves. Some congregations fully support their LGBTQIA+ ministers and other religious professionals; others, even if they are not intentionally discriminatory, still behave in ways that create a toxic work environment, making those professionals feel uncomfortable, unwelcome, and perhaps even unsafe, and obstructing their work.

More than one person declined to share their story for this project because it felt unsafe to "go public" with what had happened to them in a congregation or in our denomination.

While this book focuses on Unitarian Universalism within the United States, one of our tasks must be to recognize that LGBTQIA+ Unitarians and Unitarian Universalists in other parts of the world may experience much more discrimination, and even persecution. For example, in Transylvania, Unitarian churches face state pressure to not support gay marriage, which is still deeply controversial there. In Uganda, the situation is even worse: the 2023 Anti-Homosexuality Act includes penalties including life imprisonment and the death penalty.

We must continue to support LGBTQIA+ congregants, ministers, and religious professionals of all kinds, whether they participate in brick-and-mortar congregations (in the US or elsewhere) or in online communities such as the Church of the Larger Fellowship. After I published an article on coming out in the June 2019 edition of *Quest*, the CLF newsletter, I received mail from incarcerated CLF members who have to remain closeted for their own safety.

Speaking of safety, many of us in the LGBTQIA+ community have feared for both our civil rights and our safety in recent years.

My wife and I got legally married in October 2020, shortly after the appointment of Amy Coney Barrett to the Supreme Court, because we were afraid that federal recognition of marriage equality might be overturned. I know we were not alone in that. In recent years, many states have passed a deluge of anti-LGBTQIA+ legislation, often specifically targeting trans people, especially trans youth. With the inauguration of a second Trump administration in 2025, the federal government is also targeting LGBTQIA+ folks, especially trans+ people.

We are also still the targets of violence. As I prepared to submit an earlier draft of this book to Skinner House in November 2022, there was a shooting at Club Q, an LGBTQ+ nightclub in Colorado Springs, Colorado, which left five people dead and twenty-five more injured. The day after that shooting was the annual Transgender Day of Remembrance, when we lament the transgender people who were murdered for being who they were. That day's shooting was just one example of many I could list in recent years.

I wish stories of hardship for LGBTQIA+ people, both within our denomination and beyond, were only part of history, not the present, but we have not yet come close to achieving that goal. I dream of a future when this book, and all those other stories not held within these pages, will in fact be a part of our history that must be told, but no longer a current reality.

The title of this book comes from something Rev. Victoria Safford said to me and my wife the day after she preached at our wedding. Although the impetus for our marriage was our desire to protect ourselves as best we could from the ongoing homophobic backlash, we had focused our ceremony not on our peril but on our love for each other, and she described us as "defiantly joyful." We loved the phrase so much that we chose to have it engraved inside our wedding rings. Not every story in these pages has been joyful, and not every story expresses defiance, but those two characteristics embody much of what I have learned from the contributors to this book: that our existence can be, and for now perhaps must be, both defiant and joyful. In the long term, I pray that the defiance will no longer be necessary, and that we may more easily lean into the joy.

Appendix

UUA General Assembly Social Witness Statements

Over the last fifty-five years, the delegates to the UUA's General Assembly have passed a variety of social witness statements related to LGBTQIA+ rights, welcome, and inclusion.

- 1970 General Resolution: Discrimination Against Homosexuals and Bisexuals
- 1973 General Resolution: Creation of an Office on Gay Affairs
- 1974 Business Resolution: Office of Gay Concerns
- 1975 Business Resolution: Office of Gay Concerns
- 1977 Business Resolution: Gay Human Rights
- 1980 Business Resolution: Ministerial Employment Opportunities
- 1984 Business Resolution: Gay and Lesbian Services of Union
- 1986 General Resolution: Opposing AIDS Discrimination
- 1987 Business Resolution: Supporting Legal Equity for Gays and Lesbians
- 1989 Resolution of Immediate Witness: The Travel Rights of HIV-Infected People
- 1989 General Resolution: AIDS/HIV Crisis

- 1989 Resolution: Proposals of the Common Vision Planning Committee to establish the Welcoming Congregation Program
- 1992 Resolution of Immediate Witness: Opposing Legalization of Discrimination Against Gays, Lesbians, and Bisexuals
- 1993 Resolution of Immediate Witness: Acceptance of Openly Lesbian, Gay, and Bisexual Persons in the United States Military
- 1994 Resolution of Immediate Witness: Support the Employment Non-Discrimination Act of 1994
- 1994 Resolution: Sexuality Education in Public Schools
- 1996 Resolution of Immediate Witness: Support of the Right to Marry for Same-Sex Couples
- 1997 Action of Immediate Witness: Support for Non-Discriminatory Corporate and Other Business Policies
- 1999 Resolution: Work to Change Discriminatory Policies of Boy Scouts of America
- 2002 Action of Immediate Witness: Québec's Union Civile Law Passes Giving Same-Sex Couples Full Legal Equality
- 2003 Action of Immediate Witness: Global HIV/AIDS
- 2004 Action of Immediate Witness: Oppose Federal Marriage Amendment
- 2007 Action of Immediate Witness: Pass the Employment Non-Discrimination Act with Transgender Inclusion and Protection
- 2007 Responsive Resolution: Confronting Gender Identity Discrimination
- 2007 Action of Immediate Witness: Repeal "Don't Ask, Don't Tell"

- 2008 Action of Immediate Witness: Oppose the Florida and California Marriage Protection Initiatives
- 2009 Action of Immediate Witness: Oppose Sexual Orientation and Gender Identity-Based Violence in Iraq
- 2010 Responsive Resolution: Confronting Sexual Orientation and Gender Identity Discrimination
- 2011 Responsive Resolution to the Report of the President
- 2014 Action of Immediate Witness: UUA Support for 'Uganda New Underground Railroad' to Safely Extract LGBTQ People from Persecution in Uganda
- 2016 Action of Immediate Witness: Stop the Hate: Protect and Support our Transgender and Gender Non-Conforming Family
- 2021 Action of Immediate Witness: Defend and Advocate with Transgender, Nonbinary, and Intersex Communities
- 2023 Action of Immediate Witness: Organizing for Health Equity
- 2024 Business Resolution: Embracing Transgender, Nonbinary, Intersex and Gender Diverse People Is a Fundamental Expression of UU Religious Values
- 2025 Action of Immediate Witness: Defending LGBTIQ Freedom Amid Funding Crisis: A Call for Global Solidarity

Acknowledgments

So many people were part of this project, beyond the authors who contributed to the book. I can't possibly name them all, but here are a few of the folks to whom I owe a deep debt of gratitude:

Thanks to the Unitarian Universalist Retired Ministers and Partners Association, who began the UU Rainbow History Project which led to this book, for all of that work and for choosing me to shepherd this book as part of it. Special thanks to Diane Miller, who was UURMaPA Board President in 2019, when this all began. Thanks also to the many attendees at UURMaPA's two 2019 conferences who added material to the handwritten timeline on the walls or contributed material to the website. Though the website material is not reproduced in this book, it informed my work and gave it context.

Huge thanks to Alex Kapitan, who brainstormed, researched, and supported in countless ways throughout the project's long journey to publication—and especially for painstaking work on the timeline and other historical context; that section of the book has Alex's fingerprints all over it, and is far better for it.

Thanks to Mary Benard at Skinner House Books for seeing the promise in this project when it was just a proposal, and for seeing it to completion despite all that has happened along the way, including a global pandemic and the rise of authoritarianism in our nation. It has been quite a journey!

Last but not least, of course, thank you to everyone whose words appear in this book. Your stories matter, and I am grateful that you have entrusted them to me and to Skinner House so that they can reach a wider audience!

About the Contributors

Rev. Wendy Bartel and Rev. Lynn Gardner live and serve as co-ministers in Schenectady, New York. Together, they find inspiration through music and poetry, time in their garden, participating in vibrant worship, collaborating for justice, sharing delicious food, and dismantling white supremacy and hetero-patriarchy. They are humbled by the power of trust, vulnerability, and courage in congregational settings, community organizing, and family life.

Dr. Helen Bishop looked after around eighty UU congregations in the Midwest as District Executive. She served in the Peace Corps in Ethiopia; is a credentialed religious educator at the master level; has a master's degree in genetic, medieval and Renaissance music, and distance learning; and has a doctorate in organizational leadership. She has taught at Starr King School for the Ministry and at Meadville/Lombard Theological School and has worked for The Mountain, a UU center near Highlands, North Carolina. She was awarded the Angus McLean Award for Excellence in Religious Education in 2008. She and her wife, Susan Grider, have five children and ten grandchildren, and she also loves to sing!

Rev. Kimberley Debus is a Unitarian Universalist minister based in Takoma Park, Maryland, inspiring an artful and art-filled faith. She consults with congregations and religious professionals throughout the denomination and teaches courses and workshops on worship, theology, and hymnody. In addition to her consulting ministry, she also serves the Cedarhurst UUs in the greater Baltimore area. Her work as a consultant and a performing artist affirms her passion and commitment to liberation and radical welcome.

Rev. Thomas Disrud has served as Associate Minister of the First Unitarian Church of Portland, Oregon, since 1995. He is the church's pastor and a member of the executive team and has other ministerial responsibilities. He is a graduate and former Board Chair of Starr King School for the Ministry. He plans to retire in June 2026.

Rev. Jane Dwinell is a retired UU minister who specialized in helping small congregations survive and thrive. She served two small congregations as well, along with being a hospice chaplain. She is the author of four books, including *Big Ideas for Small Congregations* and, more recently, *Alzheimer's Canyon: One Couple's Reflections on Living with Dementia*, co-written with her late husband, Sky Yardley. She currently lives in a small eco-village in southwest France.

Rev. Gail R. Geisenhainer is Minister Emerita with The First Unitarian Universalist Congregation of Ann Arbor, Michigan. She and her life-partner, Celeste DeRoche, are retired in southern Maine, where Gail is currently devoted to the cultivation of queer joy through reading Sapphic Romance.

Rev. Mr. Barb Greve has made service to Unitarian Universalism his life's work, from his years in the UUA's Office of BGLT Concerns to his widespread leadership in support of religious professionals to his service as Co-Moderator for the UU Association of Congregations. Cofounder of Transgender Religious professional UUs Together (TRUUsT) and the Association of UU Transitions Professionals, Barb has served on the boards of Starr King School for the Ministry, Meadville Lombard Theological School, and the

UU Studies Network. Having served as an interim director of religious education and as a hospice chaplain, he now serves as the UU Ministers Association Director of Ministries and Programs. He is a master-level credentialed religious educator (UUA) and a certified chaplain (BCCI), serving as an Affiliated Community Minister with the First Parish in Framingham, Massachusetts.

Rev. Dr. Gwendolyn Howard has earned graduate degrees in religion, ministry, and social work. In 1980, she married Patricia Falcon. Together, they've lived in various places over the years, the longest being in Providence, Rhode Island. One aspect of ministry that took place since the writing of the sermon presented here was "Queer Vespers," a weekly online interfaith service she led for two years during the COVID-19 pandemic. Now retired, Gwendolyn and Pat (along with two happy black cats) live in an apartment in Chicago with a ten-minute walk to Lake Michigan.

Rev. Dr. Myke Johnson is a retired UU minister, having served First Parish in Brewster, Massachusetts, and the Allen Avenue UU Church in Portland, Maine. She is the author of *Finding Our Way Home: A Spiritual Journey into Earth Community* (2016) and writes an ongoing blog of the same name. She identifies as a white, working-class lesbian, now with chronic illness, and lives with her partner Margy Dowzer and their two cats. She holds a master of divinity degree from Chicago Theological Seminary and a doctorate in ministry from Episcopal Divinity School.

Zr. Alex Kapitan is a community minister, educator, writer, consultant, and activist who supports people in more deeply living their values and helps congregations to become places of radical welcome for all. Cofounder of the Transforming Hearts Collective, a faith-based

LGBTQ+ social justice organization, and founder of Radical Copyeditor, an anti-oppressive language project, Alex previously worked at the national headquarters of the UUA supporting anti-racism and Welcoming Congregation programming and has served on numerous faith-based LGBTQ+ leadership bodies, including the steering committee of TRUUsT, the organization of trans UU religious professionals.

Rev. Dr. Jonipher Kūpono Kwong currently serves as Interim Lead Minister at First Parish Unitarian Universalist in Arlington, Massachusetts. Jonipher, who is of Chinese descent, was born and raised in the Philippines. Most of his adult life was spent in California and Hawai'i with brief stints in Orlando, New York, and Toronto, Canada. He has served as a minister at the First Unitarian Church of Honolulu, the Fourth Universalist Society of the City of New York, First Unitarian Congregation of Toronto, and UU congregations in Sepulveda and Temecula Valley in California. He has also served Metropolitan Community Churches in Honolulu and Orange County, California. He worked for the UUA as the Ministerial Credentialing Director and Congregational Life staff for the Pacific Western Region. Raised with an ecumenical background, Jonipher values pluralistic religious experiences, having been christened at a Gospel church, baptized as a Chinese Mennonite, and a member of the Honolulu Mindfulness Community, a sangha influenced by the Zen Buddhist monk Thich Nhat Hahn.

Rev. Manish Mishra-Marzetti serves as senior minister of the First Unitarian Universalist Congregation of Ann Arbor, Michigan. He has served extensively in denominational leadership, including as co-chair of the Board of Trustees of the Unitarian Universalist Service Committee, a member of the Board of Trustees of the Unitarian Universalist Association, and president of Diverse Revolutionary UU

Multicultural Ministries (DRUUMM). He is co-editor of *Justice on Earth: People of Faith Working at the Intersections of Race, Class, and the Environment; Conversations with the Sacred: A Collection of Prayers;* and *Seeds of a New Way: Nurturing Authentic & Diverse Religious Leadership.*

Helen "HP" Rivers is a graduate of Starr King School for the Ministry, where they studied trauma and religious leadership and earned their master's degree in social change. They are an experienced writer, editor, and religious educator and the proud owner and operator of Blessed Bee by HP Rivers (an online Unitarian Universalist gift shop) and the Blessed Bee Mutual Aid Fund for UU Religious Professionals. They live in Appalachia with their family and love baking, crafts, gardening, photography, and spending time in nature. They are a queer, pagan, neurodivergent Unitarian Universalist pastor and proud mom to one human child, two cats named Rumi and Danny Dancer, and one hot mess of a dog named Luna.

Eric Schuman is a member of the Unitarian Universalist Congregation of Salem, Oregon, where he serves as a lay minister. UU by choice since the age of fifteen, he served as the president of the Prairie Star District and the UU Fellowship of Topeka, Kansas. After retirement, he attended Starr King School for the Ministry as a special student. A retired physician associate, Eric lives in Salem with his husband of forty-five years, along with Kimber and Archie, golden retrievers who volunteer as certified therapy dogs with hospice clients, hospitalized patients, incarcerated persons, and Indigenous high school students.

Rev. Aija Simpson-Newbury is the Minister of the Unitarian Universalists of Petaluma, California. Aija was raised in the faith and the movement and is proud to continue the tradition of lesbian parenting that her moms pioneered. When not at work, she can most often be found with her wife and child reading, building robots, and adventuring.

Rev. Laura Smidzik currently serves as Assistant Minister at First Universalist Church of Minneapolis. She served Merging Waters UU Congregations for eight years prior. She spent a decade working in higher education at Twin Cities colleges in the area of career development and a decade volunteering in leadership and as staff at Rainbow Families and Project 515, two statewide LGBTQIA+ organizations.

Rev. Dr. Sandra Szelag earned a doctorate at the University of Chicago Divinity School and the Meadville Lombard Theological School and was ordained by the First Unitarian Universalist Church of Chicago. Questions eventually brought her to Tucson, where she fell in love with the desert, stayed to raise children, and worked as a pastoral counselor. She returned to her lifelong love of words and poetry and served as a docent at the University of Arizona Poetry Center. He life could be measured by the many roles she played: teacher, activist, minister, pastoral counselor, poet, dog lover, spouse, mother, and grandmother. She lived with her spouse, Carol Kells, for forty-five years and had four children. Sandra died in 2023.

Rev. Virginia Wolf is an eighty-one-year-old white, female, lesbian, retired Unitarian Universalist minister. She is Minister Emerita of the Unitarian Universalist Fellowship of Eau Claire, Wisconsin. She and her spouse, Carol Schumacher, were lead plaintiffs in a successful challenge to Wisconsin's ban on same-sex marriage. She has come out to come home.

Rev. Jami A. Yandle serves as the UUA's Transgender Support Specialist in the Office of the Vice President for Programs and Ministries, offering spiritual care and guidance for trans and nonbinary communities within and beyond the UUA. A nonbinary minister and Board-certified chaplain based in Texas, Rev. Yandle draws upon wisdom in parish ministry, hospice chaplaincy, social justice advocacy, and conflict engagement with the UUA Hope for Us Team to help foster connection, healing, and resilience in the communities they serve.